All the White Friends I Couldn't Keep

"Poignant, urgent, and spot-on . . . In a narrative that is part memoir, part manifesto, and part how-to, Henry brilliantly weaves together his encounters with anti-Blackness and his political awakening with powerful observations about how nonviolent struggle can confront and transform racism. Don't miss this profoundly important book."

—ERICA CHENOWETH, author of *Civil Resistance*

"As a queer-, Black-, woman-identifying American who has lost many white friends since my own personal racial and political awakening, this book made me feel seen and gave language to that peculiar and silent heartbreak I've experienced."

—TINA STRAWN, co-host of *Speaking of Racism*

"Andre Henry offers up his whole heart in this compelling mix of memoir and manifesto, which clicks the necessity of revolution into clarity like a new pair of glasses. *All the White Friends I Couldn't Keep* is essential antiracist reading."

—LAUREN DUCA, author of *How to Start a Revolution*

"*All the White Friends I Couldn't Keep* combines personal stories with cultural reflection and a dash of history to create a book that unlocks the complex and makes it understandable. From his journey as a Black man in the South to his journey of living life in a Black man's body while the headlines and the country roil, Henry makes a compelling argument for the truth-telling power of anger and the extraordinary response of nonviolence to racism. It's accessible for those new to the racial-justice conversation, but so deep and nuanced that it provokes veterans of the movement to deeper reflection."

—NIKKI TOYAMA-SZETO, executive director,
Christians for Social Action

"An incredibly generous book . . . Andre Henry rips aside the veil and gives the reader a look at his journey in what is one of the most vulnerable and open books I've ever read. He takes us from his childhood in the shadow of Stone Mountain and American white supremacy to his present-day fight for racial justice and revolution. He weaves in and out of his own story, our national story, and the great thinkers that helped him become a freedom fighter. The whole time he brings the reader along with a gentleness and kindness that is sure to move and change everyone it reaches without pulling a single punch."

—JOSHUA POTASH, teacher and organizer

"The powers that bind us are not simply 'out there' in the structures of society, but also inside us in the myths we inherit. Those shared stories shape us, whatever the color of our skin. But Andre Henry has given us all a gift by inviting us along to see and hear what it means for a Black man in America to break free from the lies of whiteness. Follow him to freedom."

—JONATHAN WILSON-HARTGROVE, author of *Revolution of Values*

"Andre Henry has given us a gift of authenticity, of meaningful challenge, and of a great unburdening: he offers stunning insights on what we must release in the pursuit of liberation, so that we may labor toward radical change while remaining rooted in love and wholeness. Pay attention to him—he will surely emerge as one of the greater voices of our time."

—RAQUEL SARASWATI, diversity, equity, and inclusion expert
and Philadelphia NOW Woman of the Year

"Andre Henry is a student of what works, and he has done the work to banish white supremacy's spiritualities, strategies, and subtle psychologies that demand, 'It has to be this way.' Andre writes like he sings; he tells the truth, transmutes pain, and makes your body move to an exodus beat."

—JARROD MCKENNA, social-change educator
and co-founder of *InVerse Podcast*

"*All the White Friends I Couldn't Keep* is an insightful, thoughtful, horrifying, frustrating, and ultimately validating look into the impact of being Black in white spaces. It is a must-read for anyone who is coping with navigating faith and friendship in the age of antiracism."

—ALLY HENNY, antiracist commentator and public theologian

"Don't you dare put this book down. Learning from Andre Henry is a gift. Prepare to be enraged and enlightened, reprimanded for your complacency and redeemed by responding to the call to action. This book is for you. Don't you dare put this book down."

—REV. ROBERT W. LEE, author of *A Sin by Any Other Name*

All
the White
Friends
I Couldn't
Keep

All the White Friends I Couldn't Keep

HOPE—AND HARD PILLS TO SWALLOW—ABOUT FIGHTING FOR BLACK LIVES

Andre Henry

CONVERGENT
NEW YORK

Published in the United States by Convergent Books, an imprint of Random
House, a division of Penguin Random House LLC, New York.

CONVERGENT BOOKS is a registered trademark and its C colophon is a
trademark of Penguin Random House LLC.

Library of Congress Cataloging-in-Publication Data

Names: Henry, Andre (Musician), author.
Title: All the white friends I couldn't keep / Andre Henry.
Description: First edition. | New York: Convergent, [2021]
Identifiers: LCCN 2021052964 (print) | LCCN 2021052965 (ebook) |
ISBN 9780593239889 (hardcover; alk. paper) | ISBN 9780593239896 (ebook)
Subjects: LCSH: Racism—United States. | African Americans—
Social conditions. | Equality—United States. | United States—Race relations.
Classification: LCC E184.A1 H4586 2021 (print) | LCC E184.A1 (ebook) |
DDC 305.800973—dc23/eng/20211029
LC record available at lccn.loc.gov/2021052964
LC ebook record available at lccn.loc.gov/2021052965

Printed in the United States of America on acid-free paper

crownpublishing.com

9 8 7 6 5 4 3 2 1

First Edition

Book design by Caroline Cunningham

To Sam

You are nobody's token

CONTENTS

PART III: SINGING THE FUTURE

A WARNING FROM THE AUTHOR

Dear Reader,

    My friend told me, "You don't write a book to express yourself. You write a book because you care about your people." In that spirit, I need to alert you to something about the book in your hands: this won't be an easy read.

This book is the story of a political shift in my work and my life as an artist, triggered by the movement for Black lives over the last decade and the lessons I've learned through that awakening about the struggle for racial justice. The story of that awakening is punctuated by several lethal encounters between Black Americans and the police. This book recounts several stories of Black people victimized by police violence as well as the secondary trauma I experienced in witnessing or hearing about their deaths. These things were difficult to relive in the writing of this book, and I'm certain they will be hard to read.

I've made my best effort to retell the stories of some of the Black people we've mourned in the Black Lives Matter era without sensationalizing or unnecessarily going into the gory details. Nevertheless, it's important to me that you make an informed decision about reading the contents of this book. If you do continue, I hope that by the end of this read, you'll feel that I've cared for you well in this.

At the same time, this book is not all grief and trauma. Hope and joy have become important to me as I've engaged in the movement for racial justice, and I've given special attention to those as well. So be assured that this journey ends with joy.

I've recounted the events in these pages to the best of my ability, but I ask for your patience and forgiveness for those places where I may not remember the granular details of some events. In my effort to protect the identities of the white friends I couldn't keep, I've changed their names and other details about them that might make them identifiable. Throughout the production of this writing, I've relied a lot on my catalog of original music to organize my thoughts. I've included excerpts from three of my most relevant tracks to organize this journey through my story. Each of these songs came to me during the intense time of grief and political awakening I write about in these chapters.

I hope this book leaves you with clarity about the obstacles that lie ahead on the road to freedom, confidence that we can overcome them, and at least a little bit of laughter.

With love,

Andre

PART I

A Little Apocalypse

It must be good to be you,

You only believe what you want. . . .

—"DELUSIONAL"

Written just after the 2016 election

1

Embracing the Apocalypse

As a boy, my greatest fear was that I'd live to see the end of the world—a fear I'd absorbed by spending time with my grandma. Mumma kept her TV on all day, but she only watched a Christian station called the Trinity Broadcasting Network. Every week, I'd sit cross-legged on her bedroom floor and watch TBN's roster of charismatic televangelists parade across their gaudy stage, explaining the ins and outs of the coming end of days. They used charts and diagrams. They spoke of stars falling to earth, the moon turning to blood, and dragons and monsters emerging from the sea—weird, I know. They warned that a charismatic, anti-Christian world leader was coming to establish and preside over a one-world government, followed by seven years of something called "The Great Tribulation." The Tribulation years were predicted to be the last years of human history. But the most frightening of their end-times prophecies concerned something they called the Rapture.

The Rapture was an end-of-days event in which millions of

people would suddenly vanish—yes, exactly like the plot of HBO's *The Leftovers,* in which 2 percent of the world population disappears without explanation. But unlike the disappearances in *The Leftovers,* the televangelists could tell you exactly why the Rapture would happen. They said it would happen because Jesus was taking all the "born-again" Christians to heaven, to save them from the coming Tribulation. Christians who were left behind would be beheaded by the Antichrist's henchmen.

The Rapture was the most terrifying thing in my nine-year-old life—scarier than when my big sister Myra made me watch as she danced along with zombie Michael Jackson to the "Thriller" music video; scarier than the hissing, flying cockroaches that broke into our home on Georgia's sticky summer nights; scarier than the dark itself. My legs were still short enough to dangle over the plush red pews at Mumma's church as I sat next to her to watch a grim play in which government agents stormed into churches to kill Christians who'd missed the bus to Heaven. The thought that I could be one of those left-behind Christians haunted me every night.

I was a credulous child. I believed the televangelists were right because somebody let them talk on television, and my grandma endorsed them by nodding along while they spoke, grunting in agreement. So I woke every morning with a very real feeling that this could be the day people vanish. Routine disappearances turned into red-alert Rapture checks. If my older brother took out the trash without telling me, I'd dart around the house to make sure he hadn't been reduced to a pile of clothes. (The raptured always leave their clothes behind in the movies. I guess heaven is full of naked people.) Other times I would go check Mumma's room to see if she was there. Because if Mumma was still in her room, I reasoned, Jesus couldn't have taken anyone yet. I had nightmares about being left behind, about hiding out in stuffy, tattered, abandoned sanctuaries as the sound of soldiers' boots crescendoed past.

One night, I sprang from my bed after one of those dreams and sprinted to Mumma's room in terror, my feet *pap-papping* against our hardwood floors.

"Wha do you?" she asked with her eyebrows raised. (She always spoke in patois, as though she'd migrated from Jamaica earlier that same day.)

"I'm scared I'm going to be left behind, Mumma," I squeaked while I gripped the sheets at the edge of her bed. "I don't want to miss the Rapture."

Mumma paused. Her brow wrinkled. She looked at me with a fire in her eyes that had burned the fear of death ages ago.

"Just aaask Jesus fi tek you bifou di time come," she said.

So that's exactly what I did. Every night, I'd lie on my back in the dark, my Mickey Mouse covers pulled over my head, asking Jesus to please just do me a solid and protect me from the Apocalypse, repeating my prayer until my heartbeat calmed and I fell asleep.

Little did I know, despite Mumma's reassurances and my prayers to the contrary, I was destined to live through an apocalypse of sorts. But it would be very different from the one the televangelists predicted—more earthy and political, more concerned with the present than the future, more about new beginnings than endings. It would be more about transforming the world than escaping into the heavens.

The apocalypse I'm talking about is the ongoing movement for Black lives.* Thanks in large part to the protests of millions of ordinary, organized, outraged people, the world is in the throes of a great reckoning with death-dealing systems of racial oppression and those who uphold them. The rallying cry coined in the wake of Trayvon Martin's death in 2013—*Black Lives Matter!*—has evolved into uprisings from Bristol to Bogotá, from Johannesburg to West Papua. We've witnessed the toppling of Confederate statues, multitudes of protestors blocking traffic and surrounding police stations—all demanding an end to the state violence whose ancestry can be traced back to the colonizer's gun and the slaveholder's whip. But the work is far from done.

White nationalist counterrevolutions are stirring around the globe, seeking to stop the movement for racial justice in its tracks. If we want the latest wave of racial justice protests to culminate in a decisive victory against white supremacy—meaning the end of injustices like voter suppression, migrant abuse, imperialist wars, and police brutality—then the movement for Black lives must be strengthened and expanded. That work begins with a political awakening from the ignorance that pervades Western culture about what racism is and how it works, due to centuries of systematic miseducation in the Western world about how their societies were built.

---

* When I use the terms *Black Lives Matter* and *the movement for Black lives* throughout this text, I'm usually not referring to any official organization under these names. I use these terms as umbrellas for all social movement groups working for racial progress. I also use *antiracist movement* and *the movement for Black freedom* or *the movement for racial justice*. When referring to a specific organization, I'll use its full name, e.g. "Black Lives Matter LA."

And because most people don't know what racism is, they don't know how to fight it. This is even true of the millions of people who've taken to the streets because of the death of George Floyd, who haven't yet taken the time to study the history and anatomy of racist systems—or the movements that have prevailed against such systems in the past—and therefore think protest alone creates systemic change. The notion that marching and chanting in great numbers is the key to social progress is a symptom of our miseducation. Until we understand that nonviolent struggle is a martial art and work to master it, we'll keep commemorating the deaths of the fallen and past uprisings with symbolic actions that have no effect on the material conditions of the oppressed.

This means that, for many, the fight for racial justice begins with a wake-up call that demands we unlearn the whitewashed histories we were taught in school and in national myths repeated by politicians, preachers, and pundits. A wake-up call that disabuses us of the sanitized stories of past nonviolent movements that gut them of their radical ambitions and disruptive power. And wake-up calls are what apocalypses, and this book, are all about.

We get the word *apocalypse* from an ancient Greek term that means "to reveal" or "to unveil." An apocalypse grabs you by the shirt collar and shakes you out of the slumber of apathy and inactivity. Several millennia ago, it was a well-known, deeply political literary genre that used dramatic imagery and symbolic language. The most famous of these ancient writings is the biblical *Apokolypsos*, rendered "Revelation" in English.

Revelation was written by a man named John, a political prisoner living in ancient Rome. He wrote *Apokolypsos* to intervene against a troubling rise of flag-waving for the Roman Empire in his community, which was in the occupied province of Asia Minor. The empire had impeccable branding. They called their regime *Pax Romana,* meaning "the peace of Rome," even though said peace was established through violent military conquest. They established a cult around Caesar, through which the people Rome colonized came to deify the emperor as a savior instead of recognizing him as a war criminal who sent soldiers to kick in their doors, drag their neighbors off to captivity, burn the countryside, and raze places of worship to heaps of rubble.

The capital gave special attention to provinces with cultic centers, and influence in provincial life was linked to participation in the local cult. Its influence could be seen in the provinces' architecture and sculptures, in shrines to the empire and sacred festivals. They even inscribed it on their coins, which addressed Caesar as "Our Lord and God."[1] What made the cult such an effective means of indirect rule was that it allowed John's neighbors to envision themselves as participants in and partakers of Pax Romana instead of its victims, making patriots of the oppressed.

John wrote *Apokolypsos* to expose Pax Romana as a big lie. In this book, he depicts Caesar as a many-headed monster instead of a handsome god. He exposes the empire as a violent agent of chaos instead of peace. His message to his readers is clear: Resist.

I wrote this book because similar interventions are needed in the present. Today's empires continue to transform marginalized subjects into spokespeople. After a presidential term that emboldened white nationalists around the globe, Donald Trump became *more* popular with some minority communities than when he took office in 2016. Twelve percent of Black men and 36 percent of Latino men voted to reelect Trump in 2020, the highest numbers of Black and Latino support for a Republican candidate in over a decade.[2] That kind of support—where oppressed people are so entrenched in national myths that they clamor for their oppressors—is exactly the kind of support an apocalypse aims to disrupt. I once needed that kind of intervention.

I blush to admit that pre-apocalyptic Andre didn't see racism as being endemic to American society. I once believed racism was primarily an emotional attitude rooted in ignorance, an irrational hatred for people based on their skin color. There was a time I believed the myth that America is a fair place where people get what they deserve. I assumed that if I just conducted myself in a "respectable" way, I'd never have to worry about being jailed or choked to death by a police officer. I believed these things because these myths are part of America's version of Pax Romana—*Pax Americanus,* if you will—that the U.S. is a paragon of democracy and the leader of the free world and that racism isn't nearly as big a problem as it used to be. Needless to say, I didn't do much freedom fighting when I believed those things.

I'm willing to confess the naivete of my nonrevolutionary former life because I know I'm not the only Black person to have ever sidestepped the revolution. In 2015, after activist Bree Newsome was arrested for removing a Confederate flag from a South Carolina statehouse to protest a white supremacist mass shooting, a childhood friend of mine, a Black woman, posted a long defense of the proslavery symbol. "The Confederate flag just reminds me of home," she said. I scratched my head at her. No Black person can actually be home under the Confederate battle flag, but if we're indoctrinated with the myths of the white world, we can think we're partakers of a table we're not invited to.

I hope that my story of political awakening in this book will speak to people like the friend I've mentioned above—people with too much faith in the white world and too little knowledge of the power we have to liberate ourselves. I'm living proof that the amount of melanin in our skin doesn't automatically inform us of the true nature of our freedom struggle. So, while I'm sure a great number of people from different backgrounds can benefit from reading what's in these pages, this book centers Black political awakening.

I want to say clearly to my Black siblings that the white world has tried to keep us ignorant of the severity and scope of racial violence and preoccupy us with strategies for racial progress that will never work. They've worked hard to make us into patriotic slaves, and they've been somewhat successful in doing so: just look at the number of Black MAGA avatars on Twitter, or Black pastors fanning the flames of white hysteria about Critical Race Theory, or Black YouTubers claiming that to acknowledge systemic racism is to have a "victim mentality." Those are some of the most extreme examples of how white supremacy convinces people—even Black people—to oppose the Black freedom movement. But there are more subtle examples.

A friend, a Black woman, once asked me if we should stop identifying as Black altogether because focusing on race leads to victimhood. Another friend, a Black woman, once told me that some of the most iconic civil rights activists in history regretted their activism at the end of their lives; therefore, we shouldn't go protesting in the streets. "All we need to do is love," she said. I've had countless conversations with Black men who seem convinced that a coffee conversation with their white bosses holds more potential for change than a workers' strike.

One way or another, the white world tries to convince people—even Black people—that there's no need to organize for racial justice like Black Americans have always done. No need for disruptive, nonviolent action like the lunch counter sit-ins or the Freedom Rides of the Civil Rights Movement. They want all of us under the spell of Pax Americanus (or Pax Whatever-anti-Black-regime-you-live-under). My hope is that this book will do for my people what John hoped *Apokolypsos* would do for his. If we want to push racial progress further than it's ever gone, we must embrace the apocalypse that defies the lies we were raised on.

Today, I write as a student of nonviolent struggle for social progress. When I'm not busy producing music, I teach proven principles of nonviolent civil resistance to people around the world. I also work with local activists to build strategic nonviolent campaigns in my neighborhood. I spend most of my time and energy on this kind of work because if we want to make Black lives matter, my years of study have convinced me that millions of ordinary, organized, outraged people will have to plan and execute disruptive, militant, nonviolent campaigns for racial progress on a regular basis until our vision for a racially just society is realized. In a word: what we need is a revolution.

People often squirm when I use words like *militant* and *revolution*. It sounds extremist. But I was convinced of this approach by history's most famous proponent of nonviolent direct action: Dr. Martin Luther King Jr., a self-identified "extremist for love." In his last years, King spoke of a "revolution of values," telling a Stanford University audience in 1967: "I'm still absolutely convinced that nonviolence, massively organized, powerfully executed, [and] *militantly developed,* is still the most potent weapon available to the black man in his struggle in the United States of America." King was the first of many voices who convinced me that a militant, nonviolent approach to racial progress is necessary (not to be confused with militarism, which he condemned). Nonviolent direct action is militant in that it is active, confrontational, strategic, and disruptive against systems of oppression. It's combat. But unlike conventional warfare, this method avoids physical harm to the opponent.

Nevertheless, I get why people find all this conflict language—combat, opponents, confrontation, militance—off-putting. We don't want to be at war. But I'll tell you what I often tell others: you may not like to think in terms of war, but if you're Black, the white world is already at war with you. The race war has been raging since the day Europeans began to massacre and enslave indigenous people, and it continues today in everything from the racial wealth gap in the United States to the unequal impact of the climate crisis in the Global South. And, I know, it's not fair, but we must either fight back or submit. I say we overcome the organized violence of this anti-Black world with organized nonviolent resistance of our own. In this way, militance isn't about being aggressors. It's about self-defense.

There's no workaround for the revolution. Black freedom

won't be achieved through one-on-one coffee discussions with racists, diversity hires, interracial relationships, time, love, panels on racial justice, or education alone. Only revolution will save us. But I didn't always believe America needed radical change.

I was once that kid with an odd love of country. I remember lying on my bedroom floor, legs kicking behind me, as I filled white, glossy poster boards with charts and tables showing the significant events of the American Revolution: The Boston Massacre, the Boston Tea Party, the Battle of Saratoga. The story of how the colonists stood up to the bully King George and demanded their freedom—fought to the death for it against an empire—arrested my imagination and sent electricity running through my little veins. That was the America I knew: the land with revolution in its DNA, the land with Lady Liberty anchored at its gate saying, "Give me your tired, your poor, your huddled masses yearning to breathe free." I believed in *that* America. And I thought the only revolution that America needed was the one that freed it from British rule.

It wasn't easy for me to conclude, years later, that racism was part of the cake of American society, as opposed to a fly nibbling at the icing. It was like losing belief in God or having your heart so broken that you are closed off to love. I didn't want to believe that racism was alive and well in the country I loved—more deeply entrenched, more pervasive than I'd ever imagined. But, as they say, the facts don't care about your feelings.

I had so many feelings about this, though. There were many afternoons when I'd drop whatever book I was studying and weep over the crimes my country had committed and hidden. On some nights, I'd fall on the floor, groaning in tears over the friends who had turned on me for speaking up about those crimes. Somehow, my efforts to share the truths I was learning about our country was interpreted by them as hate: hate for them as people. Hate for America.

The irony. I'd begun this quest out of patriotism. It's just that the more I learned about American history, the more the world I thought I lived in—the one where racism was pretty much in hospice—slowly vanished. The apocalypse, that great unveiling of the world that renders us awake to monstrous political realities in the present (and inconceivable future possibilities), had come.

And with the apocalypse came the part I once feared most. People began to vanish from my life. Many of them were cherished friendships with deep roots, but those bonds proved to be brittle as I began to speak up about racism and revolution.

I grew up in the American South, in the world of white evangelicalism. I attended their churches and youth camps, trained for ministry at their schools, preached at their churches. For a long time, I felt like a beloved part of that world. At one point, I even imagined myself making a career in it; maybe I'd start a church, or write Christian books, or teach theology. All of that changed—my relationships with them, my relationship with Christianity, even my life ambitions—as I embraced the antiracist movement. I was surprised to see some of the people I loved most become my most ardent opponents. When I began looking for my place in that necessary revolution, most of my white friends at the time made it their business to stand in my way.

I was surprised by this. I'd always assumed that if those former white friends had lived through a revolution for racial justice—the Civil Rights Movement, for example—they would have been on the front lines beside their Black loved ones. Beside me. But the apocalypse would reveal many uncomfortable truths to me about white America through those relationships. Namely, that most white people are too deeply entrenched in anti-Blackness, and too invested in white power, to be good neighbors to Black people or valuable partners in the pursuit of racial justice.

I don't just mean white people who use the N-word or march in white nationalist protests. I mean well-meaning, I-don't-have-a-racist-bone-in-my-body white people, who nevertheless cross to the other sidewalk when they see a Black man walking toward them, or call the police on Black folks for doing suspicious things like barbecuing in a public park, or let the N-word "slip" through their lips when they get angry enough. White people with "plenty of Black friends" who nevertheless bristle when their daughters bring a Black man home. White folks who would die if labeled racist but also feel America needs saving by men like Donald Trump.

The sad truth about white people, the apocalypse taught me, is that most of them are too attached to the notion of their racial superiority to cheer, much less fight, for racial progress. Some of them would be horrified to know that about themselves; others, I learned, were plenty content with that fact. When I realized that the white people I loved would probably never join the movement for Black lives, I had to leave those relationships, because movements aren't built with immovable people. But with every friend I lost, I gained something: an apocalyptic lesson, a piece of practical insight for nonviolent revolution, or a new-found freedom to be my best Black self.

In the wake of the global antiracist uprisings of 2020, many people are at a similar threshold. Fascist sentiment is rising around the globe, and people who care about racial progress have spotted their loved ones marching in the counterrevolution to preserve white power. People are asking how these divisions can be overcome. But no such unity can be achieved—that's the hard, apocalyptic truth. Racists and antiracists can't build a new world together. Their visions are fundamentally incongruent. It's time to wake up to the true nature of this problem we call racism and to the arduous work it will take to confront it in a meaningful way.

This book won't provide any advice on how to convert racists to antiracists. Nor will it help you build bridges with white supremacists, even the benevolent ones. This book is about walking away from those kinds of people and joining those who are trying to expand the global revolution for racial justice. This is your invitation to embrace the apocalypse. But I'm warning you: once you are awake, you'll never go back to sleep. Welcome.

2

The Whole World Is Stone Mountain

I was raised in the shadow of Confederate Mount Rushmore, in a small Georgia town called Stone Mountain. The place gets its name from a giant piece of quartz that stands about a mile high at the edge of town. The mountain's north face hosts the largest bas-relief carving in the world: a giant depiction of Confederate generals Robert E. Lee and Stonewall Jackson and Confederate president Jefferson Davis on horseback. It was commissioned by Klan sympathizers who'd initially hoped to include a parade of Klansmen in the carving. At 190 feet across and 90 feet tall, it's the largest Confederate monument in the country. The modern Ku Klux Klan first set fire to a cross on that very rock.

One Fourth of July, my sweet mother, a hardworking immigrant, took my siblings and me to picnic at Stone Mountain Park. As night fell, she spread a blanket on the damp grass at the mountain's base, and passed around half-frozen Capri Suns as we prepared to watch the famous "Laser Show Spectacular," where the generals go dark, and fast-paced cartoons are projected against the mountainside to popular music.

As the show began, Mom—"Mackie," we called her—couldn't stop grinning. She leaned in close with a smile and said, "There's a part where they make the soldiers move!" She seemed as excited about the imminent resurrection of General Lee as most Americans are about the fireworks' grand finale. I was excited, too, imagining a kind of *Night at the Museum* situation, where those stone sentinels would peel themselves away from the rock and dance to the Kris Kross song "Jump."

After a few cartoons set to country songs I was too young and Black to recognize, the show paused. The lights dimmed. The sound of a rolling snare drum came dragging its feet through the speakers. It was followed by the voice of Elvis Presley, singing, "I wish I was in the land of cotton, old times there are not forgotten! Look away! Look away! Look away! Dixie Land!" As the music crescendoed, a laser began to slowly trace the carved figures until they were all standing in multicolored, stenciled glory.

Then, the flickering silhouette of General Lee—I kid you not—turned his gaze on us mortals below, put on his hat, kicked his horse, and began to ride. Jackson and Davis followed, as Elvis changed choruses: "Glory, Glory, Hallelujah! His truth is marching on!"

At first, the three men's steeds took a dignified pace. Then General Lee spurred his horse into a gallop, and the other Confederates followed suit. Lee drew his sword and held it high above his head as the three rebels turned toward us in full-on charge. The sound of hundreds of people hooting and clapping and cheering filled the air.

In hindsight, it seems odd that people would commemorate

America's birthday by applauding three men who once declared war on the country. Even odder is the memory of my Black mother wriggling her hips at the thought of a family picnic on the very ground where the KKK was resurrected—all while "I Wish I Was in Dixie" played in the background.

If Mackie had recognized the laser show for what I do now— white supremacist pageantry—she might have marched our family right out of that neo-Confederate theme park and across the Caribbean Sea in a fury, to raise us in her home country. But none of us were furious, because we didn't really know the history. There was no mention of the ties between Stone Mountain and the Klan in Stone Mountain Park. They covered it up.

In Stone Mountain, the racist content of mundane American life was obscured by a big lie told throughout the white world.

The lie the white world tells is, "Racism is not a problem here"—no matter where "here" may be. White people from the southern U.S. claim they're not racist because they're not members of the Proud Boys. Northern whites claim they aren't racist because they're not Southerners. European whites claim they're not racist because they're not Americans. Latino whites claim they're not racist because they're not Europeans *or* Americans. Nevertheless, the white world stands guilty of a crime of unfathomable scope.

Some call it the *Maafa,* a Swahili word meaning something like "Great Disaster," referring to the fifteen million indigenous Africans violently abducted from their homelands to be sold as beasts of burden in the so-called New World. They were held as captives in work camps, tortured and terrorized for generations;

their descendants have continued to suffer through endless innovations of racial violence throughout history—including apartheids and poverty, police brutality and surveillance, imperialist wars and outright terrorism. The *Maafa's* body count is innumerable. That's why some Black scholars call it the Black Holocaust.

Contrary to what people love to say about racial violence—that it springs from ignorance or blind hatred—the *Maafa* wasn't, and isn't, senseless. The crime was undertaken for a reason: profit. Over and over again, in their writings about the slave trade, white men spoke of how they must use the sweat and suffering of enslaved Africans to build their banks and textile industries, their ships and plantation homes, and to produce whatever else they "needed" to buy or sell: their coffee, tea, sugar, rum, cotton, indigo.[1] It was just business.

Much of the world is implicated in the crime and the cover-up. Britain couldn't have become "Great" without their work camps in Jamaica, but British schools don't spend a lot of time teaching about the violence the British Empire wrought in its colonies. In 2005, the French government tried to pass legislation that urged schools to emphasize the "positive role of colonialism," while schools glossed over the Black rebellion that ended French enslavement in Haiti.[2] Brazil sweeps its history of anti-Black ethnic cleansing under the rug of "racial democracy," suggesting that the same country that once ran the world's largest slave market now has little to no racism. In 2018, the Southern Poverty Law Center (SPLC) surveyed students from one thousand high schools in the U.S. and found that fewer than half of them had ever heard of the Middle Passage.[3]

My point is that complicity in this atrocity is as widespread as the denial. The many nations who've benefited so much from the *Maafa* lack the moral courage to confess that the breaking of Black bodies is a central part of their stories. They're unwilling to appraise the damage or to make whatever reparations are possible, making the suffering of the marginalized of their societies inevitable and invisible to those who have no desire to see it.

Malcolm X once asserted that "America is Mississippi" to say that the nation couldn't write racism off as a Southern problem. I'm saying the whole white world is Stone Mountain in that it tries to write off anti-Black racism as a uniquely American phenomenon, when it really is a *global* catastrophe. The signs are right in front us, mountainous in scope, but they remain shrouded by the big lie.

These nations that are built and maintained by racial hierarchy tell the big lie to prevent revolutions. The powers that be know revolutions begin when ordinary people conclude that their situation is unjust.[4] So if they can convince people that racism isn't a problem, then governments can spend less money on rubber bullets to shoot protesters, corporations can spend fewer resources on hiding slavery in their supply chains, and ordinary people can excuse themselves from the annoyance of reflecting on their racist behavior.

There's a term to describe how the white world tries to keep us from perceiving the racism that pervades the Western world: gaslighting. Gaslighting is such a buzzword that I wish I knew a better term for what I'm describing. I don't. It comes from a 1938 play by Patrick Hamilton called *Gas Light* in which a man meddles with his wife's gas-powered lights and tells her they're only flickering in her head. The point of gaslighting is to get the target to doubt their own perceptions of reality and accept the gaslighter's interpretation.

That's what the white world is trying to do to us: on the systemic level by hiding history (like how Stone Mountain Park hid its Klan ties) and on the interpersonal level by telling Black people we're just being too sensitive or paranoid about racism being a serious problem. The white world wants us to repeat the big lie after them: *raaacism iiiizzz nooot a prooooblem heeerrrre.* Learning to call bullshit on the white world's racial gaslighting was my first apocalyptic lesson—a lesson we must all learn to move racial progress forward. For me, learning to call bullshit began as a slow process of learning to see through the lies.

The white world's gaslighting was strongest for me when I lived in the shadow of Confederate Mount Rushmore. In my hometown, the white world's big lie took the form of a mind-bending cocktail of Lost Cause propaganda and colorblind racism.

After the Civil War, ex-Confederates worked to reframe their proslavery coup as a justified uprising against tyranny. Organizations like the United Daughters of the Confederacy pushed for school curricula that taught that the war was really about states' rights, not slavery. Southern states incorporated the Confederate Battle emblem into their flags, as a symbol of pride. Monuments to Confederate leaders were built, venerating those traitors as heroes. This grand cover-up set the stage for a pervading ignorance in my hometown about the antidemocratic elements that have always existed in America's politics. But this ignorance was fueled by another key development in the mid-twentieth century.

When the Civil Rights Movement made overt racism taboo, white supremacists pivoted to colorblind rhetoric to maintain white dominance. Former Republican National Committee chairman Lee Atwater broke it down in an infamous 1981 interview:

> You start out in 1954 by saying, "Nigger, nigger, nigger." By 1968 you can't say "nigger"—that hurts you, backfires. So you say stuff like, "forced busing, states' rights," and all that stuff. . . . Now, you're talking about cutting taxes, and all these things you're talking about are totally economic things and a byproduct of them is, blacks get hurt worse than whites. . . . [5]

Atwater admits that colorblindness was used by white racist politicians as a Trojan horse to preserve racial hierarchy. But American public schools don't include confessions like Atwater's in their history curricula. So most Americans have had little exposure to the ways racism evolved between 1968—the year the Civil Rights Movement began a severe decline—and the present.

All of that is to say, by the time my former white friends and I came to occupy the land where the KKK was reborn, the stage was set for our miseducation. Hidden history and colorblind delusions allowed them to truly believe that everyone was equal now and that talking about racism was unnecessary. As a kid living in the shadow of Confederate Mount Rushmore, this was the air I breathed.

Whenever I heard Black adults speak about race in the presence of white people, whether it was Black pain or Black pride, white people complained. When I overheard grown Black folks lament the 1992 police assault of Rodney King, their white friends grumbled: "Why does everything always have to be about race?!" As Februarys came and went, I sometimes heard white people moan: "How come there's no White History Month?" They insisted that if white people couldn't walk around saying "white power," Black people shouldn't be walking around saying "I'm Black and I'm proud." Race is only important to racists, they claimed.

Their favored solution for Black suffering was to stop talking about race altogether. The reasoning went something like: "Seems like you're upset a lot 'cause of racial stuff. Maybe you'd be happier if you stopped focusing so much on being Black or white or whatever, just be a human being, ya know?" It sounded good in theory, but my own lived experiences in that same community seemed to signal that race actually was consequential.

Sometimes teachers seemed to speak harsher when telling Black students to stop talking in class. Police officers used more force when stopping Black kids, and shopkeepers seemed more vigilant about watching Black youth in their stores. But whenever I tried to name those discrepancies to white people, it was like I was standing in front of a movie projector. My confessions threw a shadow across their delusions of racial progress. They demanded I sit down at once. I learned to bite my tongue, for the most part, for fear of being accused of "playing the race card." This was the dynamic between my white friends and me well into my college years.

In the years I abided by white people's reprimands, I lived in an uncomfortable state of ambivalence about my Blackness. On one hand, I wanted to be like those freedom fighters I'd read about—Harriet Tubman, and Dr. King, and Bob Marley, who publicly condemned white supremacy and rallied Black people to rebel. I especially wanted to be like Bob Marley, whose music I discovered in my parents' vinyl collection, and fight racism with music. "Get Up, Stand Up," "Buffalo Soldier," "I Shot the Sheriff"—those were my jams! I was in sixth grade when I wrote my first song with all original lyrics and music—a rap song called "Oppression" that told much of the story of Black struggle at the time, from slavery to the present. But I was convinced by the white people in my life that there were no more revolutionary battles to fight. I settled into the grammar of colorblindness. "I'm not Black; I'm Jamaican," I remember saying to a classmate in grade school. I didn't want to disappear into a generic racial category; I wanted to be special—an individual, a human being, like white people claim to be.

It's interesting how that desire to "just be human" often puts one in the company of more white people. By my college years, I was a full-blown token Black guy. You know the one—the nerdy one who gets told by his white friends he's not *really* Black because they're not afraid of him (everyone knows real Black men are scary). And if I'm honest, I think I internalized all that white approval. I wore the fact that some white folks thought of me as "not like those other Blacks" as a shield for a long time. But life in the real world would hack at that shield until it wasn't worth carrying anymore.

The gaslighting effect began to wane a few years after I left the South after college.

I moved to New York City with hopes of making it big as a singer-songwriter. I crashed at my aunt Winnie's home in the Brownsville area of Brooklyn and landed a day job as a music leader at Glad Tidings Tabernacle, a hundred-year-old church a few blocks south of Times Square. On weeknights, I'd stay out till the wee hours of the morning, singing at open mics to promote my music and sell tickets for upcoming shows.

It was the era of stop-and-frisk, a policy stemming from a 1968 Supreme Court case that allows police officers to detain anyone they find suspicious and search them for a probable cause for arrest. Between 2002 and 2013, *The New York Times* reports, the New York Police Department performed five million such stops.[6] It looked as arbitrary as it sounds. I'd descend the crowded subway stairs after work and see a line of police on the other side of the turnstile, ready to stop people; often, I would go downstairs and see more of them standing around on the subway platform, waiting to catch any "suspicious" activity.

"Virtually all of the people stopped were young African American and Latino males," reported legal scholar Paul Butler.[7] "A young male citizen in Brownsville got seized and searched about five times a year. Less than one percent of these detentions resulted in arrest." The mayor at the time, Michael Bloomberg, justified the special attention Black and brown people received by saying we were more likely to commit crimes. Simple as that.

I remember being stopped, searched, and questioned several times in my last year in New York City alone. I'd long left Brownsville for Harlem by then, but it hadn't made a difference as far as police attention goes. The first time, I'd spit on the subway tracks while waiting for the N train in Union Square, and cops approached me demanding my I.D. so they could check my criminal record. Another time, as I stood in a crosswalk waiting for the light to change with a number of other pedestrians, two cops singled me out and threatened to arrest me. Yet another time, I was on my way home from a gig with two friends when the cops pulled us over—I still don't know why—and made us get out of the car, insisting that I'd hidden a gun under the passenger seat.

As I said before, Northern white Americans love to act as if racism is a Southern problem, but my time in New York truly showed me how racism continues to thrive. When I decided to move to Harlem, I spoke to a landlord on the phone who seemed elated and impressed. "I don't meet many decent people around here," he whispered. He even said he hoped we might become friends. But as I approached the glass door of the Dunkin' Donuts where we agreed to meet, his face melted with disappointment. He refused to rent to me, even though the only thing that had changed was that he'd seen me in person.

Racial profiling was a normal experience for me in New York. I remember cab drivers refusing to pick me up. "I'm not going to Brooklyn," one cabbie yelled at me through the window. Of course, I wasn't going to Brooklyn.

It was like the whole city believed crime followed Black people. Harlem had police towers with floodlights illuminating major intersections. Patrol cars were stationed every few blocks. Officers in riot gear occupied some of the subway stations. Only two other neighborhoods in Manhattan seemed as heavily occupied while I lived there: Times Square, where there were occasional bomb threats, and Ground Zero, where the Twin Towers once stood. At times, it felt like the police occupied Harlem as though they were containing a threat. New York was different from Stone Mountain in that no one chastised me for making these observations. But if you were a Black person trying to find a home or just go about your daily business, the underlying reality was the same.

The killing of Eric Garner, in the summer of 2014, ripped a tiny hole in the thinning fog of white lies that enveloped my common sense at the time. Mr. Garner had just broken up a fight while on his way to Buffalo Wild Wings in Staten Island when two police arrived on the scene and accused him of selling loose cigarettes.[8] Garner insisted he hadn't been selling "loosies" that day, but the officers continued to hurl accusations at him, until Officer Daniel Pantaleo grabbed Garner by the neck and pulled him to the ground in a chokehold—a move that had been banned by the NYPD. "I can't breathe," Garner protested, as more cops appeared on the scene and piled onto his body. Eleven times he protested: "I can't breathe." Those were his last words.

I was more than grieved when I heard about Garner's death. There was something deep inside of me that took it personally. It was like those movies where someone breaks out of a trance momentarily. The little Andre who loved drawing pictures of the American Revolution and writing songs about Black history broke through the gaslighting fog; he was livid. I sat in my darkened office at the church with my guitar in my trembling hands and began to sing about what Garner's death made me feel, as tears left salt at the corners of my mouth:

O say, can you see?
We're all not safe in the land of the free.

It was the first time I'd even tried to write a song about racism since the sixth grade, and the first time I can remember really feeling free to call bullshit on America's lie that racism was long gone, though I only felt so free in that one private moment. I wouldn't perform that song for another three years, and I wouldn't begin even *saying* what I'd expressed in that song for another two.

A week or so later, three Black women at Glad Tidings put together a Saturday event about something called "whiteness." I'd never heard the term before. At a church staff meeting, the lead pastor cautioned that the event needed to be announced carefully so as not to cause too much of a stir. Once the announcement was made, I felt like a child watching grown-ups argue about something I wouldn't get till I was older. The event was kind of like that too.

That Saturday discussion was unlike any race discussion I'd experienced before, in that it didn't try to explain Black suffering by talking about "broken" Black families, sagging pants, and the alleged corrupting influence of gangsta rap music. The conversation that day focused on white people: namely, on the societal consequences that follow when people believe that they're white. That was entirely new to me.

They talked about the landmines Black people navigate every day to avoid the wrath of colleagues and bosses and in-laws who believe they're white. They used words like *privilege, systemic racism,* and *accommodation,* all new terms for me that described familiar experiences. For instance, I'd never thought about it as a privilege that some people generally don't feel nervous around the police, but once they explained the term, I recognized it as perfect language. Even so, I didn't go around repeating those things immediately. I just sat with the information.

I left New York later that year for Los Angeles with the term *systemic racism* added to my vocabulary. I didn't understand how the system worked, but I could see it working in the patterns of Black death that surrounded me: Black person is killed by police, the victim's toxicology report or something else is released (to say the victim was no angel, of course), protests erupt, an investigation is launched, the officer is acquitted, more protests. It happened that way almost every time, as if some algorithm was narrating the plot of each story. I eventually grew tired of my white friends acting like they couldn't sense the violent rhythm of Black death in the news cycle. They constantly asked questions like, "How do we *know* racism was a factor?" So I started speaking up about my experiences of racism online, hoping to expose that pattern. I thought if my white friends heard the truth about racism from someone who'd been stopped and frisked in several cities around the country, someone who'd been searched for drugs and weapons many times, someone they knew and trusted, that it would expose the white world's big lie—racism isn't a problem here—for the farce that it is, a little apocalypse of sorts.

I would eventually begin using social media to tell stories of some of my experiences, as proof that racism was real and causing serious harm to real people. That's where I began to lose people.

I finally recognized the gaslighting was happening even to me in the spring of 2015, when a white woman named Sherry suddenly reappeared in my life on social media.

I'd met her when I was a teenager. She was married to one of the youth group leaders at my home church in Stone Mountain. We hadn't seen each other in ages. Though we were never close, she held a place in my memory that any respected youth leader would.

She reached out to me just after I dipped my toe in the waters of posting about racism on social media.

Around that time, a young man named Freddie Gray was killed by six Baltimore police officers. Mr. Gray had been minding his business that day when he saw Baltimore Police and took off running, which the officers found suspicious. He ran, not because he was guilty of any crime but because he was wise. He'd been arrested before for things as trivial as "having gaming cards, dice."[9] So he ran to avoid their usual harassment.

When the police caught up to Gray, they noticed a knife clipped to his pants and violently put him under arrest. (Later they claimed the knife was a switchblade, which would have been illegal—had they been telling the truth.) The video footage of the arrest is a gruesome display of stop-and-frisk brutality. The officers are caught folding Gray in dangerous contortions before dragging him into a police van. Gray died in police custody after suffering severe spinal injuries.

In response, outraged protesters burned police cars, smashed windows of local businesses, and pelted Baltimore police officers with rocks. Black Lives Matter protesters filled the streets around the country.

I was distraught as I watched this story unfold in the news.

With a quivering lip and shaking fingers, I expressed my anger on Facebook with a poem:

> *I am a black body*
> *standing at the edge of space*
> *neither seen nor heard*
> *Violence! I shout*
> *Injustice! I cry*
> *The darkness drinks my voice*
> *as stars glow in the distance—impervious, apathetic—*
> *and think me mad . . .*

That's when Sherry pulled up, with poetry of her own. "I feel like because I am a white star. I have no choice, no voice," she wrote in response. I scratched my head at her. Did she just make my post about Black death about her white feelings? She did. I felt it was inappropriate, but I was afraid I might offend her by saying so. *Okay, Andre. De-escalate*, I thought to myself.

"I only meant to refer to some of the really frustrating and painful conversations with people who don't seem very interested in hearing what I'm trying to convey to them about my experience with racism. I hope I didn't make you feel like I'm referring to all white people. I'd hate that," I replied. Sherry answered with more poetry about her white woman woes, ending her lengthy stanzas with: "If you are going to describe by color, you WILL also divide by color."

In the weeks that followed, I began posting about racism on Facebook a little more often, maybe once or twice a week. Sherry was overly active in the comments on those posts, usually undermining whatever I'd written. But she wasn't the only one who took issue with me. I received a few direct messages from a few disgruntled white former college classmates, and it was getting exhausting. "I had no idea I went to college with so many racists," I vented in a Facebook post.

"But honestly Andre . . . are they all racist . . . ?" Sherry responded. "Or they just don't see everything the way you do? Racist is a really big, and often loaded, word."

When I read that comment, it finally occurred to me that Sherry hadn't been so disruptive in all those previous conversations by accident. She'd been trying to undermine the conversation the whole time. With tears gathering in my bottom eyelids, I wrote back to her: "I love you, but you're not hearing me." Then I hit the block button.

Clicking "block" that day felt loaded. I'd never blocked anyone because of some social issue before. Up to then, I thought that talking to ignorant opponents of racial justice movements was what I was supposed to be doing. But it was clear that, at least in this case, it wasn't working. Moreover, it was becoming a personal nuisance to me.

I couldn't articulate why it felt necessary at the time, but I can now: Sherry was gaslighting me. By now, I've heard some version of her question enough times to know that when she asked, "But *are* they racist?" she was really challenging my ability to perceive the world accurately altogether.

Common gaslighting tactics include denial, minimizing the target's feelings, and flat-out lying.[10] Some common symptoms of being gaslighted are having a sense that something's wrong you can't quite put your finger on, wondering if you're being too sensitive, and feeling like everything you do is wrong.[11]

When I study the tactics and effects of gaslighting, I don't just recognize exchanges between individuals like Sherry and me (although they certainly count). I hear a chorus of white people suggesting that Black people imagine racism where it doesn't exist. I also hear a multitude of young Black and brown girls who at one point wished their naturally kinky hair would become straight and blond, Black men who don't want to talk about times they've been profiled for fear of being diagnosed with a case of victim mentality, and the protests of Black youth in redlined neighborhoods who are mad at the world for reasons they can't fully explain. When I zoom out from the exchange with Sherry, I see that she's just one individual agent of a much larger system that refuses to tell the truth about racism. I see that groups can be gaslighters, and that groups can be gaslighted.

The white world has abused Black people through economic exploitation, political disenfranchisement, and social degradation for centuries. And they've used racially biased media, fraudulent school curricula, slaveholder theology, and "colorblind" racist policies to gaslight us about it.

They're trying to convince us not to trust our lived experiences, so that our own analysis of our situation won't lead to a rebellion against white power. They're like protesters who fly a drone onto the tarmac to keep planes grounded. But the stakes are too high to submit to their abuse.

It would take me about a year to learn to stop arguing with the gaslighters (in a later chapter I'll say more about *how* I learned that lesson). No matter how many questions they ask, I finally realized, they're not looking for answers. They're trying to pull the rug out from under the conversation altogether. Better to save our energy, call bullshit, and keep it moving.

Our best way to deal with the gaslighters is to strengthen our analysis of our situation without seeking their agreement. We hold fast to what we know, which includes knowledge from our personal experiences, and utilize that knowledge to create strategic plans for change. Our analysis of racism isn't for them, to try to persuade them. It's for us, because an accurate analysis of an oppressive situation is the basis for choosing wise strategies for liberation.

Civil resistance expert Robert T. Helvey, who has helped activists around the world topple dictators from Serbia to the Philippines, encourages activists to gather information about all the factors that may affect their struggle for justice in a similar way that conventional armies prepare for battle. This includes everything from the topography of the area where their campaigns will take place, to the laws that could impact their actions, to the number of soldiers in the police force—how long it takes them to get from point A to point B, and in what order.

Many people who laud the Civil Rights Movement in the United States don't realize how much time those activists spent analyzing their conflict situation before taking action, in a way that Helvey echoes. Before activists ever set foot in Birmingham for their famous sit-in and boycott campaign, they spent months analyzing their situation. In a plan they called "Project C" (for Confrontation), organizers calculated the distances between their movement headquarters at the 16th Street Baptist Church, the businesses they were targeting, and city jails; so that when one group of protesters was bailed out of jail, another group of arrested protesters would be on its way, keeping pressure on both the jail and local businesses to compel the city to take down the WHITES ONLY signs.[12]

Notice that these activists didn't go into Birmingham requesting mass meetings with white folks to convince them that our lives matter, nor did they go picking fights with random white people on the street. They were too busy strategizing a tangible disruption to Birmingham's racist system to be bogged down in meaningless confrontations with white people. They embodied the teachings of Mahatma Gandhi, who deeply influenced many civil rights leaders, that nonviolent confrontation is "literally holding on to the truth."[13] They responded to the system's racial gaslighting—the notion that all was well in Birmingham—by shutting the city down and dramatizing the problem, and it was their analysis of the situation that empowered them to do so.

That kind of work remains important in the struggle against racism today. But we'll never get around to it if we're stuck in endless debates about whether racism is a problem. This is all the more important in the wake of the "post-truth" presidency of Donald J. Trump.

We're living through an epistemic crisis of daunting proportions. On the other side of the Trump administration, agreement on what is true seems scarcer than at any time in recent memory, making it nearly impossible for people of different political backgrounds to collaborate for the common good.

Conspiracy theories, disinformation, and propaganda are exacerbating the alarming trend of democratic backsliding all around the world. White nationalists are being mobilized around the lie that nonwhite people aim to annihilate white civilization through Ethnic Studies programs and calls to defund the police.

And the powerful resurgence of the Black Lives Matter movement after the killing of George Floyd is being absorbed into
their narrative of fear.

The lies don't look like they'll subside any time soon. This
means that one of the most important things we can do for racial
progress is to call bullshit on racial gaslighting while we work on
our own analysis of systemic oppression. Today, my attitude is,
unless I and another person are fighting racism together, there's
no need for us to debate about it.

3

The Right to Remain Angry

met many of the white friends I couldn't keep at my grandmother's church, the fairly large, multiethnic, evangelical As-
sembly of God Tabernacle in Decatur, Georgia. She took my
older brother Chris and me with her every Sunday. Chris got
bored with church early on and stopped going, but not me. I
sprang out of bed on Sundays with Christmas-morning energy,
eager to find my Bible and jump into my church slacks and
button-up shirt. I loved church because it was so different from
my home life.

My parents split when I was in second grade. Mackie took
sole custody of my siblings and me. I took it pretty hard. Dad
was my hero, and I desperately wanted him to come back and
live with us. When I wasn't busy praying to be spared from the
Rapture or drawing American revolutionaries, I was figuring out
how to "parent trap" Mom and Dad back together.

Mackie was so busy working several jobs to feed us, we mostly
saw her when she barreled through the back door after work.

She made landfall with ferocious momentum: fussing about how filthy the house was or how we hadn't finished our homework. And while it was true that our homework and chores were rarely done before she got home, in hindsight I can see she was angrier at life than at us. I was too young to know what her marriage to Dad had been like, but I knew it had ended rough. Until she remarried, she managed our household by herself—four kids and her elderly mother—all while healing from the divorce. Although she was full of love, she didn't have much time for friendship with us.

My older sisters, Megan and Myra, were old enough that they felt more like aunts than siblings. They were Mackie's assistant managers: cooking meals, tutoring, picking us up from school, and a host of other parental tasks. So we weren't close. Then there was Chris, the closest to me in age but the furthest from me in affection. We were as good of friends as Israel and Palestine. He and I fought so much that Mackie feared one of us would kill the other one day.

Finally, there was Mumma, who seemed happiest in her room alone singing hymns. She had severe arthritis and the chronic pain made her kinda surly, so we gave her plenty of space. Nevertheless, Mumma and I probably had the most in common because of our religious zeal. I'd wake up at 5 A.M. on Saturday mornings to catch the Christian cartoons, like *Superbook,* that came on before the regular cartoons like *Teenage Mutant Ninja Turtles* and *X-Men: The Animated Series.* On weekdays after school, I'd put on kids' worship songs in my bedroom (or the living room, to the chagrin of absolutely everyone but Mumma) and sing and dance the breath out of my body. My siblings didn't know what to make of me, but Mumma found me endearing. It was in her heart to dance to Jesus songs, just not in her joints anymore. But sometimes, she'd join me in the living room anyway and sway a little. It was one of the rare occasions when she would smile.

All that is to say, I remember wishing I had more friends at home. I wanted my family to be closer—to have things like family dinner and game nights, to be like the Huxtables or the Winslows. Instead, I felt like I was always getting the side-eye from my sisters for liking church too much, or not understanding the concept of matching clothes, or having too high-pitched a voice.

But not on Sunday. Sunday was different. Sunday was the day Mumma and I went to go meet our friends.

She was something like a local celebrity among Caribbean parishioners at the Tabernacle. As soon as we entered the foyer, she transformed from our family grouch to the church mayor, just gliding through the space shaking hands and kissing babies. And since I was friends with Myrtle McKenzie—more than that, her grandson—her friends became my friends. They'd dote on me, giving me candies and quarters and compliments until I hid behind Mumma's skirts. In time, I came to call Mumma's friends Aunt this and Uncle that.

At church I learned I had another friend: Jesus. I can't remember what egregious sins I'd committed by the time I was seven, but when I heard Jesus died to save me from them and be close to me, I was moved to tears. I shuffled my tiny feet down the church aisle, knelt at the altar, and repeated after the children's pastor to ask Jesus "to come into my heart and be my Lord and Savior." God became the father who'd never move out of our house, Jesus the older brother who'd never bully me, and the people at church the family I felt I couldn't have at home. I mean this in a pretty literal sense: one of the families at church, the Stones, practically adopted me.

I met the Stone family at the Tabernacle when I was eight, through a program called Royal Rangers, a Christian knock-off of the Boy Scouts that met on Wednesday nights. Ben, the patriarch of the Stone family, was the equivalent of a scout leader for one of the Royal Ranger clubs. Rachel, his wife, was the same for the Girl Scouts equivalent, the Missionettes, and their four kids were enrolled in both programs.

When I found out about the Royal Rangers, I was thrilled to have another reason to go to church. One night, after a Royal Rangers meeting, Ben noticed me standing by the fountain in the courtyard waiting for a ride home. "Is someone coming for you?" he asked. I explained that there were several people who were likely to take me home—probably one of Mumma's friends. I just had to figure out which of them had come to church that night. Not having the confidence of a nine-year-old like myself, Mr. Stone decided not to leave my safely getting home to chance.

"Where do you live?" he asked.

"Just seven minutes away," I told him.

Since it would only be a small detour, he let me join the family in their pale blue minivan and dropped me off on their way home. It was the beginning of a beautiful friendship.

The car rides evolved into sleepovers at the Stones'. Their eldest son, Jonathan, and my brother, Chris, and I would stay up all night watching movies from Blockbuster, eating Pizza Hut, and playing Super Nintendo. Sleepovers at the Stones' evolved into sleepovers at Mackie's house, and sleepovers led to Thanksgiving dinners. Over the years the Stones melded into my extended family. Then, on my eighteenth birthday, we made it official. Mackie threw a rite of passage ceremony for me, affirming that I'd crossed the threshold into manhood, and she asked me to choose two sets of godparents as part of the occasion. The Stones were one of those pairs. The Stone siblings and I would regard each other as blood well into adulthood. But time—and their refusal to hold space for me as I learned to express my anger about racism—would test the strength of that bond.

In November 2014, protests broke out in Ferguson, Missouri, when a grand jury decided not to indict officer Darren Wilson for killing Michael Brown, an unarmed Black teenager, earlier that year. Accounts of what led to Mr. Brown's death vary, but most agree that it started when Officer Wilson confronted Brown and his friend Dorian Johnson for walking in the street.

"Get the fuck on the sidewalk," Wilson barked, then backed up his SUV to block their path, nearly striking the two. Johnson says the officer grabbed Brown's shirt through his open window.[1] It was a tug-of-war, Johnson says, with Brown fighting to free himself from the officer's grip. The two young men fled after Wilson fired two shots from within the car. But Wilson exited his vehicle and continued to shoot after them. At that point, Brown turned back toward the officer—and that's where things get fuzzy. Eyewitnesses say they saw a range of things: from Brown charging at Officer Wilson to Brown kneeling in the street pleading for his life, but at the time, the popular narrative was that Brown had his hands up in surrender when Darren Wilson shot him six times.[2]

The grand jury's decision outraged millions. We were tired of watching police officers dispose of Black bodies like used tissues with no consequences. We wanted accountability.

On Thanksgiving Day that year, I slipped out of Mackie's house just as the family began to put away our very Jamaican feast—complete with jerk turkey, rice and peas, curry goat, and rum cake—to congregate in the den to watch football. I was home visiting from Fuller Seminary in California. As was my holiday custom, I jetted across town to have second Thanksgiving dinner with the Stones.

I arrived to see Ben and Rachel reclined in front of their giant flatscreen TV, watching some kind of prank comedy show, too stuffed to move. "There's plenty of food in the kitchen. Please take some," they begged. I could already hear my godsiblings' raised voices as I approached the kitchen threshold. When I entered, I saw the eldest son, Jonathan; the youngest son, Connor; and the eldest daughter, Ashlee, standing by the food, talking at Ashlee's husband, Guthrie, about the Ferguson uprising.

Something you should know about Guthrie: he was whiter than any of the rest of the Stones. He had the look of someone who was born in a police uniform: tall, stocky, and bald, with a thick Southern accent. He couldn't have been older than twenty-seven at the time, and yet the Stones treated him like Drunk Uncle from *Saturday Night Live*—someone always blurting out something problematic, but so hopelessly behind the times and beyond changing you can only shake your head at him.

Once I was within earshot, I could hear that Guthrie was in the middle of an anti-Black monologue. "I've dealt with a lot of those people," he explained. He then ticked through a litany of anti-Black stereotypes to blame Michael Brown for his own death. He went on about broken Black homes, the corrupting influence of Black culture, and how Black people are just more likely to commit crimes. He seemed to conclude that Black people are the sole cause of Black suffering and should therefore stop protesting the system and go get their—our—house in order.

For a moment, fire filled my veins. My jaw tightened. I pulled my biceps back from leaping at him, like a dog on a leash. I scanned the room, looking at each of my white siblings. Did none of them hear this man basically call Black people savages?

I bit my lip for a second to calm down. Then I explained to Guthrie that unrest in cities like Ferguson stems from legitimate anger at centuries of violent oppression, not from some extraordinarily violent impulse unique to Black people. I told him that if he learned about that history of racial violence, he might understand why some Black people could be angry enough to break windows or burn things.

"You need to learn more about the white man's history," Guthrie replied.

I took a deep breath. Did this man really just wag his finger and tell me to learn about "the white man"? Black Americans spend all of grade school learning white people's history. We learned in elementary school that "in fourteen hundred ninety-two, Columbus sailed the ocean blue," but we didn't learn about how the Iroquois Confederacy modeled the democratic ideals colonizers appropriated in the Declaration of Independence and the U.S. Constitution. We read Shakespeare and Dickens and Fitzgerald in high school but weren't required to read Baldwin or Morrison. We're treated as if there's everything to be learned about white people and nothing worth knowing about ourselves.

It's hard to articulate how it felt to stand there, knowing a hundred ways to refute what Guthrie said, but feeling frozen. Knowledge doesn't move through our bodies the way it sits on this page—all organized in neat little lines. The facts I had in my head about racial history were swirling among a myriad of other charged questions: *Is this guy fucking with me right now? Does he really expect me to construct a history of Black people on the spot? Is he even speaking in good faith? This guy sounds like a racist. Am I even safe here? Do I belong here?*

My face became hot like a laptop trying to process too much code. Insert that damned color wheel spinning where my head should be. Part of me wanted to refute his argument with a deluge of facts. Another part of me wanted to karate-chop him in the throat and yell at him: *Fuck your racist, Elmer Fudd–lookin' ass!* But he was family. I didn't want to embarrass him or myself.

I sealed my teeth even tighter around my tongue. Then I scanned the room again, my eyes widening at my siblings. *Don't any of you have anything to add?* I asked with my eyebrows. No one answered. My heart sank. I took a deep breath and power-walked through the door, to my car, without looking back.

I'd bitten my tongue all evening because I didn't feel free to express my anger about racism, even *while* I was experiencing it. But the next year, the apocalypse would teach me that Black people have a right to be angry about anti-Blackness.

I spent a lot of time in the spring of 2015 trying to appear respectable to the white friends I couldn't keep. I wanted to avoid the appearance of being angry, thinking it would be more persuasive. Because once white people sense you're angry, you lose them. Just as I had with Sherry, I always responded to their racist comments with "I can see why you'd think that, but . . . ," always giving them the benefit of the doubt. I thought I had to approach my white friends like that in those days—to educate them without offending them.

The Stone siblings reemerged when the Freddie Gray riots erupted in Baltimore the following spring. They were much more vocal on Facebook than they'd been months earlier at Thanksgiving dinner, and not on my behalf. I had posted an article from a Black, independent news source reporting that only one percent of the Baltimore protesters were breaking windows and setting things on fire—about one hundred people of an estimated ten thousand.[3] "Those 10k people should be stopping the 1000 idiots and standing for the community," Connor Stone, the youngest son, posted about the protesters. He went on, railing about how bad parenting was the source of the riots. I actually chuckled at his comments at first, because when I looked at Connor, I still saw the fluffy little man-cub he'd been when I first met him in the Royal Rangers. His comments seemed like he was repeating something he'd overheard grown folks say at dinner. Nevertheless, I engaged him. "Martin Luther King Jr. once said 'a riot is the language of the unheard,'" I replied. I explained how the Baltimore riots couldn't be understood apart from the War on Drugs, racial profiling, and broken windows policing.

"The media is stirring up all this racial division so the government can impose martial law," he said. I humored him, explaining that the media wouldn't be able to race-bait anyone if racism weren't a real issue. He didn't seem to find my reasoning compelling.

It took years for me to recognize that this conversation was the same one I'd had with his brother-in-law Guthrie months before, just more polite. Connor knew better than to insinuate that Black people were savages or to tell me to research "the white man's history," but the beats of the conversation were identical. White guy suggests there's just something inherently wrong with Black people; I try to reason with him or point out a factor he hasn't considered; white guy doesn't recognize that he doesn't know as much about the subject as I do. But this exchange was just the tip of the iceberg: it explained why the Stones didn't correct Guthrie months before. They agreed with him. They wouldn't have expressed themselves like he did, but Guthrie had said out loud what they felt deep down: something is inherently wrong with Black people. Maybe it's our culture or broken families or bad parenting—they don't know—but something ain't right.

I'd always assumed that my god-siblings had been trying to correct Guthrie before I'd crossed the threshold of their kitchen, the previous Thanksgiving Day. But now I'm not sure. Who's to say that they weren't passionately agreeing with each other before I walked in, and my presence was the only thing rendering them silent?

The Stones seemed committed to not understanding the anger on display in Baltimore, using the riots to either denigrate Black people in general or to undermine the movement. No matter how gently I tried to push back on their racist ideas, I found my courtesy wasted on them.

Not long after my run-in with Connor, his older sister, Ashlee, reached out via direct message to reprimand me for saying I understood the Baltimore riots. "Andre, when I was a minor, I was [assaulted] by a black man who nearly took my life. . . . I'm not looting and burning down my city nor feel the need to," she wrote. "There's no reason for it no matter the root issue. . . . You're my brother and I love you, I love everyone but for you to say you don't condone but understand why they would is kinda not cool."

I hated the fact that she'd been harmed in that way, but something felt infuriating about the way she was trying to use her story to silence the anger of an entire people group.

"Just because you don't understand something doesn't make it wrong," I replied. I was trying to be as short as possible because I wanted the exchange to end.

"When did u become so angry?" she retorted.

"I'm actually not angry," I wrote back.

"Lol. Ok," she replied.

I lied when I told Ashlee I wasn't angry—I just didn't know it. I'd been angry for as long as I could remember, from the day I came to recognize what it meant to be Black in this country, but I'd been trained to feel like rage was off-limits—so well-trained that I believed myself when I told Ashlee I didn't have any rage. I didn't yet understand how anger at injustice could be a healthy and productive emotion.

Angry is a loaded term for us because we know how rare it is for white people to respect it. When white people say you're angry, they're not saying, "I recognize how you feel, and that's valid." More often, they're appraising your character, naming an innate quality, a defect. Your anger isn't caused by some real, external, infuriating circumstance. You're angry in the way that bacon is salty or mangoes are sweet, "one of those perpetually angry Blacks." It's a statement of disapproval, meant to make us loosen our lips, fix our faces, and take the bass out of our voices. We're expected to speak about the injustices that threaten our bodies the way someone would read the dosage instructions on a bottle of pills. Do anything else, and you risk a range of punishments: from a white friend shutting down the conversation to an officer pinning you to the ground.

For centuries, accusations of anger have been brandished as a weapon to suppress Black rage, or more precisely, to get Black people to suppress it ourselves. American slaveholders expected their captives to be "well-behaved," which meant compliant. It was normal to hear of an enslaved person being beaten to death for "sassing" their so-called master. During the Jim Crow era, Black people were expected to abide by a strict racial etiquette that signaled our inferior status: always addressing white folks as "Mr." and "Miss," stepping off the sidewalk to make way for them, removing their hats in the presence of a white person. Faced daily with these and other forms of oppression, Black people were expected to be agreeable—or else!

When I got into trouble as a boy, sometimes Mackie would whip me with a leather strap and tell me not to cry (a habit that smacks of plantation punishment). She threatened that if I squealed because of the lash, there'd be more lashes. White America has been doing something similar throughout its history. They captured Black people and then tortured us for trying to escape. They enslaved us, then killed us for rebelling. They subjugated us, then brutalized us for protesting. Time and time again, they've abused us and then tried to pathologize and punish us for fighting back.

And yet, even as they worked Black people to death in concentration camps, burned us alive for entertainment at county picnics, bombed our cities, and treated us like animals, they somehow convinced themselves that Black people in general weren't angry about it.

Their denial of our rage spans generations. Virginia legislator James H. Gholson said in an 1831 speech: "Our slave population is not only a happy one, but it is a contented, peaceful and harmless one."[4] Around the time of the Civil War, Southern slaveholders promoted images of smiling and singing enslaved Black people to suggest that we were content in captivity: the "Mammy" and "Tom" tropes promoted images of jovial, demure, massalovin' Black folk who didn't want to be free.

Those deceptive Black caricatures prevailed over white America's imagination well into the Civil Rights era. "I never, with my eyes, saw the mistreatment of any black person," said *Duck Dynasty* star Phil Robertson, who was born in 1946, as he described pre–Civil Rights race relations to *GQ* in 2013.[5] "Not once. Pre-entitlement, pre-welfare, you say: 'Were they happy?' They were godly . . . no one was singing the blues."

African Americans were most certainly singing the blues before and during the Civil Rights era. Robertson was in his twenties when Nina Simone released "Mississippi Goddam," a response to the murders of Emmett Till and Medgar Evers and the bombing of the 16th Street Baptist Church in Birmingham—"an angry, violent song 'cause that's how I feel about the whole thing," Simone told an interviewer.[6] The song was so edgy for its time, some DJs refused to play it. But it became an anthem of the Civil Rights Movement. She sang it at the famous 1965 march Martin Luther King Jr. led from Selma to Montgomery. Simone said she was so angry after singing that song, her voice "broke" and she never sang the same again.[7]

During that same time period, Malcolm X urged an audience in Los Angeles to reject the racial etiquette of Jim Crow and tell white America "how Black people really feel, and how fed up we are without that old compromising sweet talk. Stop sweet-talkin' [white people]! Tell him how you feel! Tell him about the hell you've been catchin'!"[8] Psychiatrists Price M. Cobbs and William H. Grier explained to journalist Art Brown, "All Black people are angry. Black people in this country have had it."[9] And James Baldwin famously told a radio host, "To be a Negro in this country and to be relatively conscious is to be in a state of rage, almost all of the time. . . . It isn't only what is happening to you. But it's what's happening all around you and all of the time in the face of the most extraordinary and criminal indifference, indifference of most white people in this country, and their ignorance."[10]

Many white Americans today live in the same kind of ignorance my predecessors complained about in their time. White people are desperate to believe that Black people aren't angry, and they have their own modern happy-slave tropes to reassure them of that: their token Black coworkers, their nebulous Black friends, and magical Negroes. They've convinced themselves that racism was abolished long ago; therefore, anger isn't warranted anymore. On that basis, they treat Black rage like a rare delusion some Black people experience from dwelling too long in an exaggerated past.

At the same time, they remain just as committed to suppressing Black rage as their ancestors were. They may not use a noose or a whip to make sure Black people put on an agreeable face, but they have their means. Black rage is suppressed today by tear gas and rubber bullets in the streets, by pink termination slips at the office, and by Facebook messages to close friends telling them "it's kinda not cool" to understand why Black people riot. We're left with an ultimatum: if you want to succeed in this world, you'd better turn that frown upside down.

There's a reason the white world has tried to censor Black anger: anger is a revolutionary emotion. When the oppressed are fed up with their mistreatment, they become more likely to organize their outrage into sustained resistance against their oppressors. That's why powerful institutions and people invest immense resources to manage public outrage.

Social scientist and activist Brian Martin has written extensively on this topic. In his book *Backfire Manual,* he explains that oppressors use a common set of tactics to avoid upsetting the public: they cover up their crimes, devalue their victims, reinterpret their actions, use official channels to give an appearance of justice, and—if all else fails—intimidate or bribe their victims into silence.[11]

Black America has watched this pattern of outrage management about Black suffering for years. We've seen police plant weapons on their victims, as they did in the case of Walter Scott (cover up). Media outlets tell us drugs were in someone's system when the police murdered them, as they did with George Floyd (devalue). White people constantly try to reframe police brutality as a problem of "a few bad apples" instead of a systemic problem (reinterpret). When the grand jury refused to indict Darren Wilson for the killing of Michael Brown, that became the end of the story for eager racism deniers, though the report also showed racial bias in the conduct of the Ferguson police department (use official channels). And there isn't room for a full list of the times protesters of these injustices were met in the streets with flash-bang grenades and tanks (intimidate). Oppressors have perfected these tactics so well, they stop revolutions before they start, on a daily basis, without us ever noticing.

Rank-and-file white people also try to stamp out Black rage wherever it emerges. They tell us Black anger is destructive and can't be trusted. The truth is just the opposite.

Black rage is trustworthy because it carries an analysis of present injustices. On a physiological level, anger is the body's way of telling us that a boundary has been violated. It's the natural emotional response humans have to being wronged, especially if that wrong is recurring and denied by the harmdoers. Therefore, Black rage is a healthy sign that we as a people recognize the crimes that have been, and continue to be, committed against us. Our anger is based in our personal experiences of anti-Black hostility in the white world and backed by our knowledge of our history.

Black rage can be constructive because anger can be the starting point of hope. If anger is something like an alarm system, telling us things ought not be a certain way, then it's likely that we already hold some idea for how things ought to be. That vision of how things ought to be is the most important building block for a revolution; after all, it's hard to build a world we haven't envisioned.

That's partly why I now tell people that if they want to make a difference in the world for racial justice but don't know where to start, they should think about what makes them angry. I ask them about what keeps them up at night, what makes them go on a one-minute rant without stopping for breath. That could very well be the place to start.

I began to embrace my anger with confidence the following summer, when I stumbled upon the work of historic organizer Stokely Carmichael (later known as Kwame Ture) in a clickhole of Civil Rights speeches on YouTube—as one does. Carmichael marched with Dr. King from Selma to Montgomery, participated in the Freedom Rides that integrated interstate travel, and was part of the 1964 Freedom Summer project that led to the 1965 Voting Rights Act. By the time Dr. King was assassinated and the U.S. began its war with Vietnam, he was pissed. "This country is a nation of thieves," he announced in one speech. "It stole everything it has, beginning with black people. The U.S. cannot justify its existence as the policeman of the world any longer."[12]

I was in awe watching him speak: the ferocity in his eyes, the power in his voice. He was so defiant, incisive, and clearly uninterested in tiptoeing around white people's feelings—he was free. It was breathtaking to watch him. I remember thinking, "I had no idea we could talk like that! I want to talk like that." Carmichael became one of many models that summer—including activist Fannie Lou Hamer and author James Baldwin—who demonstrated that Black anger wasn't a hindrance to racial progress. And from that time onward, I traded coddling white people's feelings for being clear about my mission and message.

The apocalypse showed me that white people's tone policing is bullshit and that Black rage is healthy. Nowadays, when white people call me angry, I don't lie like I did to Ashlee. When I choose to respond, I usually tell them, "You're right. I am angry, and for good reason. Why aren't you?" It's good for them to encounter Black anger because it undermines the big lie that everything is all right.

Embracing my anger has also taken away that layer of mental stress that came from second-guessing my perception of reality. I no longer mull over white people telling me my anger is unfounded or inappropriate. That mental freedom gives me the confidence to stand up to their attempts to police my tone. I'm not looking for white people to pin a blue ribbon on me for good behavior, so I don't care if they call me angry as a euphemism for defective. If submitting to white supremacy is good behavior, I want to misbehave with my every waking breath.

Being honest about my anger has also helped me to manage it in a healthy way. When we deny our anger, it can consume us inside or erupt unpredictably. Acknowledging my rage has allowed me to arrange my life in such a way that it's manageable. (More about this later.)

Today, I honor and trust my anger. It was the freedom to be angry that first compelled me to begin singing, writing, and speaking about racial justice on a regular basis. Anger provoked me to show up on the streets in protest. It was the spark that started all of the work I've done over the years in the movement thus far. I know that millions of others throughout history would say the same. Their voices and stories all testify to the constructive power of anger at injustice.

More than anything else, the freedom to be angry about the

Maafa is a way Black people assert our humanity. We have a right to all of our feelings, without regard for how white people might feel about them. If the white world wants to be assured that Black people aren't angry, they should stop doing infuriating things to Black people. It's that simple.

4

The Personal and the Political

I kept my distance from the Stones for several months. When any of them reached out, I tried to make the exchanges as short as possible. I needed space to process their silence after Guthrie admonished me about white history at Thanksgiving, and even more, after they derided the Baltimore protesters after the death of Freddie Gray. I wasn't sure how to engage them once the apocalypse unveiled their anti-Black beliefs.

I missed some significant milestones for them. I missed Ashlee's baby shower. "Wish you were going to be here this weekend," she wrote to me. "We're announcing to family the gender of the baby and you're part of the fam." But I'd never felt less like "part of the fam," and I didn't want to fake it.

Nevertheless, the next time I passed through Atlanta, I arranged to join the Stones for lunch at a little storefront Mexican restaurant they liked to eat at on Sunday afternoons. The whole family would be there, including Guthrie. As I approached the restaurant doors, I rubbed my fingers against my palms to quiet my nerves. I didn't know what to expect. Would I have the displeasure to hear Guthrie pontificate on the sources of Black suffering again? Would Connor enlighten us about what white parenting methods would prevent the next race riot?

My fears melted momentarily when I locked eyes with Ben and Rachel, the senior Stones, at the front of the restaurant. We smiled big at each other and hugged. "It's so good to see you," Rachel said as she buried my face in her brown mane. Ben cracked a dad joke and patted me on the back as he opened the door for me. The rest of the Stones were already seated, snacking on chips and salsa. Guthrie sat next to Ashlee. We didn't greet each other.

As I found my seat, the senior Stones announced there'd be no talking about politics at the table. I had to pull my eyebrows back into place before anyone noticed my look. I understood Ben and Rachel's intent: they wanted to prevent another blowup like the infamous Thanksgiving I stormed out of. But I found it frustrating that their solution was to forbid any talk pertaining to race at the table. Race might have been "politics" to them, but for me it was a matter of life and death.

It became clear that day, as I washed my feelings down with tacos, that the Stones didn't have family reflexes when it came to me. We had called each other family for most of my life, yet they stood by as Guthrie, a newcomer, denigrated Black people—to my face!—without saying a word to correct him or comfort me. And their solution, later on, was to forbid me from speaking freely about my Black life. One would hope that their family would draw the line at "you will not speak to our brother that way." Instead, they asked me to watch my mouth around their racist-in-residence.

I didn't consider myself a political person at the time. Though I'd written a song or two about racism and poverty, I wasn't an avid news watcher, and I'd never voted in any kind of election either. For a long time, politics felt like the murky, complex world of lifelong professionals, most of whom were lying anyway. I couldn't perceive any drastic changes to my personal life with the transfer of Oval Office occupants, and not knowing how they affected my life made local politics feel irrelevant too.

When I'd confronted Guthrie during the holidays for speaking ill of Black people, politics never entered my mind. I thought I was talking about somebody's son lying in the middle of the street in his own blood. I thought I was talking about me being turned away from an apartment after the renter laid eyes on me. I was talking about the personal suffering of real people. But those very real experiences were written off under the abstract label of "politics."

I felt a way about how the Stones were handling this situation, but couldn't put that feeling into words at the time. I would stumble across the language I needed later that year, in a popular slogan used in women's liberation movements.

In the 1970s, Black feminists convened consciousness-raising groups* to reflect on their day-to-day lives as Black women. At-

---

* These were discussion groups with the goal of helping oppressed people see patterns of systemic oppression in their daily lives.

tendees met regularly to discuss work, sexuality, their experiences with the healthcare system, their home lives, and more. "The sessions aimed to inform members and assist them in being socially aware of issues that African Americans faced in their political climate," explained Brenda Eichelberger, who founded the National Black Feminist Organization.[1]

It may seem odd to some that Black people were holding space to make Black people "socially aware of issues African Americans face." But leading Black feminists, like the Combahee River Collective, explained that the psychological toll of oppression alone can stifle political awakening and action.[2] Bombarded with so much anti-Black hostility on a daily basis, we can often feel too depleted to think of anything beyond personal survival. These realities are why Assata Shakur wrote in her autobiography, "The less you think about your oppression, the more your tolerance for it grows."[3] It's crucial that we make space to reflect on our oppression.

Consciousness-raising groups had been the bread and butter of feminist movements because they gave women space to voice grievances about their home lives without the risk of being gaslighted by men—who often accused women who were unhappy with male dominance of being defective. Carol Hanisch, a prominent feminist voice, said that consciousness-raising groups "destroyed the isolation that men used to maintain their authority and supremacy."[4] By comparing their stories, women were able to identify the home as a site of gender oppression and see that they weren't crazy to experience it as such.

As women throughout the movement reflected on their lives together, their stories confirmed a societal pattern of gender oppression at home.* This was a subversive idea because common sense at the time suggested that issues of power didn't apply to private life. Just like the Stones implied at lunch, men were suggesting that the personal and political are separate. The slogan "the personal is political" was coined by women activists to combat that false idea: it clarifies "as social and systemic what was formerly perceived as isolated and individual," explains civil rights advocate Dr. Kimberlé Crenshaw.[5]

The personal is still political. And Black people still need spaces to reflect on our struggles to live whole and happy lives in this anti-Black world. Environmentalist Aric McBay explains: "People need time to consider their experiences . . . they need analytical tools to understand their experiences and put them in a political context, and they need people they can talk to about these things, especially a community of people with similar experiences."[6] When we're given the time and space to reflect together, we're able to recognize that our personal problems are part of a shared struggle. This creates opportunities for empathetic community, personal affirmation, mutual aid, and collective action.

A mistake some Black people face while waking up is to assume that the white people who were around us pre-awakening will hold that kind of space for us as we shake off the white world's big lies. In hindsight, I can see that I made that mistake with the Stones. The hard pill about that is white people have a

---

* Consciousness-raising groups among Black feminists added another layer of reflection that highlighted not just gender hostility from white and Black men but also racial hostility from white men and white women—even white feminist activists.

history of preventing Black people from having consciousness-raising spaces *among ourselves,* never mind participating in any kind of racial consciousness-raising space with us. For a long time, it was illegal for Black people to even congregate at all.

I didn't have all of this social justice terminology in my back pocket at the time, but I can see now that I was trying to process my Black experience in the world with the Stones, and I expected them to hold space for that, even if it meant sitting with their discomfort. I intuited that if they could really listen to my story and hear about the violence Black people live with every day from someone close to them, our alleged family could've become a consciousness-raising space for them. But I failed to consider the possibility that the Stones may have kept me around *because* I didn't make them aware of the racial violence that holds our world together. They clearly didn't want to hear how the issues they'd heard about through news or social media were affecting me personally. When they said no talking about politics at the table, they meant, "Let us eat our tacos in peace."

There's not enough plain talk about the connection between racial violence and consumer culture, so I'm glad that lunch with the Stones illustrates it. It's common for Americans to insist that there's a place and time to talk about politics, but that place is never here and the time is never now, because—you see—we're very busy enjoying consumer goods.

In 2016, Vice President Mike Pence was confronted by the cast of *Hamilton* about the Trump administration's immigration policies: separating asylum-seeking families and caging kids at our southern border. At the end of the show, the cast stood together on the stage as one member read the vice president a letter: "We, sir, are the diverse America who are alarmed and anxious that your new administration will not protect us, our planet, our children, our parents—or defend us and uphold our inalienable rights, sir. But we truly hope that this show has inspired you to uphold our American values and work on behalf of all of us. All of us."

President Trump later tweeted that the vice president had been harassed at the theater. "The Theater must always be a safe and special place," he wrote. "The cast of Hamilton was very rude last night to a very good man, Mike Pence. Apologize!"

When white people demand the privilege to sit comfortably in restaurants and theaters, football stadiums and churches, shopping malls or even on the couch, without having to consider the violence that pervades their society—especially the violence involved in the production of the goods they enjoy—they invoke a consumer-capitalist tradition that stretches back to colonial times.

By the seventeenth century, the *Maafa* had caused an economic boom in Britain's American colonies that sparked a consumer revolution throughout the empire. Now that they had more money, settlers sought a higher standard of living, buying luxury goods like tea and coffee, sugar and books. Rich settlers built lavish mansions and bought fine china tea sets to display their wealth and status. There was even a market for knock-off luxury goods among middle-class settlers wanting to be like the rich.

In the background of this consumer revolution, colonizers were putting down a bunch of slave revolts. The biggest of those revolts, the Stono Rebellion in the South Carolina colony (1739), was violently suppressed during that period; it inspired South Carolina's Negro Act of 1740, which made it illegal for Black people to assemble, learn to write, and earn money. South Carolina already had a different law, the Security Act (1739), requiring white men to carry guns on Sundays, so they would be ready to respond if the enslaved revolted while their so-called masters were at church! These violent responses to Black uprisings clarified the position of white people in society—all while making sure Black labor would continue providing the goods the white world wanted.[7] The consumer culture of that time was literally produced by systemic racial oppression and sustained by white supremacist violence.

In bringing up this history, I'm not saying that the Stones and other contemporary white people are no different from colonial militias putting down slave revolts. They're obviously further removed from the violence involved in making their running shoes and chocolate bars than the violence their predecessors used to farm sugar cane and harvest cotton. But white people today continue to reap the material and psychological benefits of living in a global system produced and sustained by racial violence. That they refuse to reflect on how their tacos make it to their lunch tables doesn't make them innocent.

Scholar-activist Paul Gorski calls the consumer habits I'm describing macroaggressions—"mindless participation in or compliance with big, systemic forms of oppression."[8] It's disregard for the people, creatures, and ecosystems who are harmed to produce the things we consume. Like many white people, the Stones wanted to macroaggress without being disturbed. They didn't want to become aware of the violence that cleared the land for the highways they drive on or the shopping malls they frequent, the violence that continues to provide tomatoes for their salsa and cobalt for their laptops, or the violence that continues to reassure them that Black people are beneath them. And peace is what they call the violence out of sight and out of mind.

The peace of the privileged isn't just about ignorance or creating space for leisure. It's also a way of reinforcing their identity as privileged people. This is a more insidious aspect of privileged peace, because in many scenarios it's their knowledge of marginalized people's suffering that makes their privilege legible, meaningful, possibly even sweeter.

Though friction exists among white people across lines of gender, class, ability, and religion, white people have often found solidarity in their efforts to bar Black people from fully enjoying what white society has to offer. Their shared contempt for Black people is one way the contours of white identity become visible. That contempt is most obvious in the breaking of Black bodies, but the breaking of bread over our bones appears to be just as important.

I say that because they seem to savor what they know of our suffering. They know that Black people, as a group, don't share the same access to wealth, healthcare, protection under the law, or political power. Yet they often recite whatever they know of those realities with smug indifference. Sometimes, white people even *delight* in our misery—consider the white kids who posted a "George Floyd Challenge" to TikTok, taking turns to kneel on their friends while one giggled, "I can't breathe." Anyone who is tempted to say they were just being kids should know that a grown-up New Jersey police officer was also fired in the summer of 2020 after organizing a kneeling protest to mock George Floyd.[9] "Comply with the cops and this wouldn't happen," one of the demonstrators shouted at cars passing by. So yes, white people of all ages get together and revel in the fact that, because they're white, they'll never know the horrors Black people protest.

As they congregate in anti-Black fellowship, white people reassure themselves of their existence. When they sit down for Thanksgiving dinner and opine about sagging pants and unwed mothers, high school dropouts and welfare checks, they're saying to one another, "I am white. Can you see me?" Every chuckle at the racist comments flying across the table says, "Yes, dear. I see you." And when they scoff about the number of Black people who are poor, incarcerated, and unhoused, they're saying, "We are the haves, and the reason 'those people' are have-nots is because they're not worthy like us, isn't that right?"

They need to rehearse these myths about their superiority to justify the imbalances of power and resources, rights and privileges they enjoy. They tell themselves they have more because they worked hard for it and for no other reason. They love to talk about meritocracies, about people pulling themselves up by the bootstraps, about self-made men. And while it's often true that many white people do work hard for what little they have, it's irrefutable that hard work alone isn't the only factor that determines a person's quality of life in this world. Yet white identity might very well unravel without these daily signals from their media outlets, businesses, governments, and even their regulardegular friends that tell them they are—to quote a famous white supremacist U.S. president—"very special" people.*

This might explain why white people are so defensive about their space. They'll insist that their dinner tables are not political. And while it may be true that they do no intentional political consciousness-raising at Sunday lunch, they nevertheless uphold and protect the dominant and pervasive anti-Black common sense of the wider society while they eat. Then they reinterpret our Black experiences—which undermine the myths they crave—as "politics," a euphemism for impolite conversation. They gaslight us and call it keeping the peace.

To the privileged, peace means keeping a safe distance from the cries of the oppressed. They can't seem to differentiate social peace from their own personal comfort. They don't seem to understand that there is no peace where there is no justice. And if we want to advance racial progress, we must disturb their peace with that very fact—that injustice and peace are mutually exclusive.

When I used to let white people set the boundaries of conversation, I thought of Black suffering as more of a personal experience. In the same way that men have told women politics had nothing to do with their experiences in the home, white people tell us that our personal experiences are unrelated to issues of political power. They conclude Black suffering is solely con-

---

* This is what Donald Trump told the insurrectionists who attacked the U.S. Capitol on January 6, 2021, in a tweeted video: "This was a fraudulent election, but we can't play into the hands of these people. We have to have peace. So go home, we love you, you're very special."

nected to personal choices—whether bad choices by individual Black people or racist choices by individual racists. And individual problems require individual solutions.

Consider the story I told about the landlord in Harlem—the one who initially offered me an apartment and his friendship but changed his mind when he saw me in person. At the time, I treated it primarily as an exchange between individuals. My solution to that problem was to just look elsewhere for housing. But if I'd understood that the personal is political, I would've recognized that some of our personal suffering is actually collective suffering that requires political intervention.

When I came to understand that Black renters in the U.S. are shown 11 percent fewer rental units than white renters, and Black real estate customers are shown about a fifth fewer homes than white homebuyers,[10] it became clear that simply trying to avoid individual racist landlords can't mitigate the problem of housing discrimination for me or any other Black person. Housing discrimination is a systemic problem affecting multitudes, linked to political issues such as gentrification, the racial wealth gap, and racist housing legislation. When we understand housing discrimination as a collective problem, we can see the need for collective action to confront it. That means impacted people can get together with their allies and organize a solution. That solution could be a get-out-the-vote campaign on important housing legislation in the next local election, packing city council meetings with disgruntled renters, starting some kind of network to hold racist landlords accountable, or even (my personal favorite) organizing a rent strike to pressure a certain landlord to meet tenant demands.

In a similar way, if we're serious about ending police violence, we can't just concern ourselves with the personal attitudes of individual police officers. We must pay attention to the billions of dollars spent to outfit police forces like domestic armies. We must change policies like qualified immunity and institutions like police unions that make it nearly impossible to hold officers accountable for criminal action. We have to pressure the media to stop producing propaganda that upholds the myth that Black people are dangerous and that more police officers keep us safe. The list goes on. Many of the decisions affecting policing are made by local lawmakers, which means we'll need to know something about local politics to address them.

This means part of the struggle for a more equitable society requires that we get somewhat political.

Political could mean attending more city council meetings, participating in local elections, or even running for political office. It could also mean volunteering with a local social justice organization, donating to one, or starting one. But political could also mean planning an occupation of your city manager's yard until they meet the community's demands. It could mean gathering with neighbors and organizing mutual aid initiatives to address food insecurity and poverty, establishing community-based mental health services or a transformative justice program to address harm between neighbors. Whatever we choose to do, we must learn to identify the structural problems that create personal suffering and then address them—otherwise we'll just be spinning our wheels.

The need for political interventions is even more salient to me today than it was that day I sat with the Stones for lunch. In the wake of George Floyd's gruesome killing, millions of people filled the streets around the world to declare that Black lives matter. Numerous books on antiracism shot to the top of the *New York Times* bestseller list. These all seemed to be signs that the white supremacist common sense that has dominated so much of the world was cracking. At the same time, I'm concerned that the big lesson many newcomers to these race conversations are taking away is that individuals have personal work to do around racial bias and prejudice. While the personal work is important, we need everyone who aspires to be antiracist to understand the importance of organizing collective action for structural changes. Systemic problems require systemic solutions.

I left lunch with the Stones that day as a full-body sigh, my shoulders heavy. *This family doesn't know how to love me*, I thought. And I broached the fact that the Stone family was not a community where I could be at ease. No, even among them, I had to be on guard against racism. I decided that day that a room where I must be quiet to make men like Guthrie comfortable is not a room I'm willing to sit in, even if my "family" is eating in there. There would be no more lunches, weddings, or holidays with the Stones. That was the last day I saw any of them in person.

PART II

The Art of Struggle

No it won't stop because we're upset,

And it won't stop because of our fear,

No it won't stop because we need rest,

It won't stop because of our tears,

It won't stop until we confess all the blood that we

spill around here,

It won't stop until we repent of all the Black bodies

broken 'round here.

—"How Long?"

Written in 2017 in honor of Tamir Rice and Sandra Bland

5

We Do Not Debate with Racists

Before that morning, I'd never seen anyone bleed to death. But on July 6, 2016, I watched with the rest of America as a young Black man, Philando Castile, breathed his last in front of his girlfriend Diamond Reynolds and their four-year-old daughter on Facebook Live.

At the time, I was finishing up a theology degree at Fuller Theological Seminary in Pasadena, California, and feeling doubtful about the prospects of building a career as a singer-songwriter. I was still playing sets in Hollywood from time to time, but studying to become an Old Testament professor had become Plan B.

I was sitting in the final course of my degree program, Beginning Greek, when I'd first heard whispers of another police killing. I told myself I wouldn't look. "I've seen too much death this year," I whispered under my breath. Just the day before, America watched Alton Sterling die at the hands of a Baton Rouge police officer. "It's not healthy to see so much death," I repeated to myself, trying to stifle a gut-churning sense of responsibility to know the news.

I ran from the sight of Castile's demise until it felt pointless to keep trying to do so. This was the kind of news you couldn't hide from. Everyone was sharing it on Facebook. Every major news outlet was covering it. Every person of color I knew was talking about it. It became clear that whenever I decided to pull my head out of the sand, he'd be waiting for me, moaning, his once-white shirt sopping wet with blood. Eventually, I caved.

"Did you just shoot my boyfriend!?" Ms. Reynolds asked Officer Jeronimo Yanez, who had just shot Castile. She tearfully recounted her boyfriend's death to her phone, to anyone she hoped might witness. She and Castile were pulled over by the police for a busted taillight, she said. After his license and registration were requested, he informed the officer of his concealed weapon, which was fully licensed. When he reached for his wallet where his driver's license was, the officer shot him. Several times.

"Stay with me!" she begged. As I watched, it was hard to know whether she was urging us watching online not to look away or begging her dying boyfriend to hang on to life.

You can hear Officer Yanez swearing at himself in the background, his voice fading as he backs away from the vehicle.

"God, please!" Reynolds repeats. The officers order her to exit the vehicle with her hands up. You can hear her daughter shriek at the sight of the police ordering her mother to get on her knees so they can cuff her. Later-released police footage would show Ms. Reynolds handcuffed with her daughter in the back of a police car. She's hysterical—understandably—as four-year-old Dae'Anna tries to soothe her. "Mom, please stop cussin' and screamin'," the child begs, "'cause I don't want for you to get shooted."

Yanez later said he stopped the family because he found Castile suspicious. According to him, Castile's "wide-set nose" fit the description of a robbery suspect.[1] But I'll never believe him. Either Yanez has telescopic cameras where his eyes should be, or he didn't get a good look at Castile's face as the car whizzed by him, because he didn't need to. Yanez could say "wide-set nose," a description broad enough to fit multitudes of Black people, and that would suffice because in America, "the description" and "Black" are synonyms.

As I watched this tragic scene, it felt like time was moving slower. I sat there in Greek class with my forehead in one hand, twisting my hair with the other, as I watched. *Who the hell cares about translating Greek verbs while my people are being slaughtered like this?* I thought. I was livid: not even the presence of his partner or their child could protect Mr. Castile, nor could his little girl's age shield her from the sound of gunshots, the sight of her own father's blood, or the knowledge of what the back of a police car smells like.

Before that day, I'd heard countless stories of the violence Black people have endured in this country. I'd even experienced some of it myself firsthand. But nothing convinced me more about the abject contempt this country has for Black life than watching the terror inflicted on Mr. Castile's family. And to know that that little girl—a four-year-old girl!—already knew to warn her mother that they could be punished for showing grief at what they'd just witnessed, tore my heart to pieces. She knew that what happened to her father could happen to her mother, to her—and she was right, that was the worst part. Any Black person who's been paying attention holds this same terrible knowledge: it could happen to any of us. And I felt that terrible knowledge again that day, that I could be Philando Castile.

I was tired of being reminded on any given day that my wide-set nose, or my dreadlocks, or my hoodie might make me fit the description. Tired of being reminded of the stigma of danger that's been associated with my complexion.

I've never felt like a dangerous person. I make my own bruschetta, for God's sake. I once landed a job as a campus security guard and quit shortly after someone caught me skipping down a hallway after hours. When I lived in New York, I walked around the city with a copy of *The Chronicles of Narnia* in my messenger bag. I don't think there's anything less threatening than a grown man who cooks homemade Italian appetizers and reads children's stories on his way to work. If only a plate of antipasto in my hands could shield me from the dehumanizing gaze of this anti-Black world. Maybe if I made sure I never left home without it, complete with a little FREE SAMPLES placard and toothpicks, it might signal to bodega owners, white ladies in elevators, and police officers that I'm not the threat they've been trained to see.

But it's been proven time and time again that no such shield exists. In a system built and fueled by Black suffering, it seems no quaint personal detail or evidence of our humanity can protect us. That Charles Kinsey was lying on his back with his hands up couldn't protect him. That Tamir Rice was a twelve-year-old boy couldn't protect him. That Mr. Castile was someone's partner and father, and that his partner and daughter were with him, couldn't save him.

One might argue, "Well, when someone first sees you, they can't see the personal details about your life. None of those details matter about anyone." But that's not true, not in America. White terrorist Dylann Roof shot and killed nine unsuspecting parishioners while they prayed at church. Officers somehow not only managed to abduct him alive but to take him to Burger King. Brock Turner, a young white man, was sentenced to only six months in county jail for assaulting a young woman behind a dumpster because the judge said a more severe punishment would have "severe impact" on the perpetrator's future.[2] And who can forget Jake Angeli, the infamous "QAnon shaman," the most recognizable of the January 6 insurrectionists, who was granted a special organic diet while incarcerated for storming the U.S. Capitol?[3]

Even when caught committing some of the most heinous acts imaginable, white men seem to retain the details of their humanity. The system still tracks their needs from the bottom to the top of Maslow's hierarchy. Yet that same system often tries to gut Black people of any such human detail.

As I watched Philando Castile breathe his last, I made several commitments to myself. First, I vowed that the news cycle would no longer determine when I talked about racism. Speaking up subtly and occasionally, as I had done up to that point, seemed to reinforce the idea that racism lies dormant between viral police killings. Second, I determined to learn everything I could about racism in our time. Third, and probably most important, I promised to find some way to involve my actual body in the struggle to end racism.

In keeping with my first commitment, I went live on Facebook almost daily, to share my personal experiences of racial profiling. There was a lot of disagreement online about Castile's death: about whether his killing was justified, whether it counted as racism. "Let's get all the facts," the white people in my life repeated. I hoped that my firsthand experiences with racial profiling would convince these people that racism wasn't as rare or hard to identify as they seemed to think.

Kevin, one of my closest seminary friends, was one of those people. In response to one of my posts, he shared an article about a white man who gave police the benefit of the doubt after an officer killed his son. "In his grief," Kevin explained, "he waited for the facts before casting judgment as to whether what happened to his son was just[ified] . . . in our outrage and grief we must be wise and make wise decisions based in facts not our emotions."

My eyes rolled so hard to the back of my head that my neck followed. Here we go again. I was sick and tired of responding to that sentiment: telling white people that one can't ignore the history that make deaths like Philando Castile's loaded for Black people. For many white people, the facts of Castile's death began the moment the police decided to stop his car and ended the moment they shot him. But we know that window is too narrow when determining how racism was a factor in his killing.

The facts are that policing in the U.S. evolved from slave patrols, established to control the movement of Black and indigenous people. Black people are about three times as likely as white people to die in a police encounter, according to a 2020 Harvard study.[4] And Castile himself had been stopped by the police forty-six times—forty-six times!—for minor traffic violations.[5] Those are just some of the facts. All of the facts cover centuries of history and millions of books. That racial history must serve as the ground of truth for the conversation. But I didn't bother trying to unpack all that information for Kevin.

By then, I'd had enough of those exchanges to recognize that this one wasn't about the actual content of Kevin's unsolicited advice. It's unlikely that Kevin lost any sleep over the details of Castile's death. He just felt compelled to tell Black people how not to respond to the event. And I just wanted the conversation to end.

"This man is not my role model," I told Kevin.

"He is mine," Kevin replied.

Since we clearly weren't seeing eye to eye, we decided that it might be best for us to discuss it over a dinner. That dinner never came, but it wouldn't be our last confrontation.

My commitment to involve my body in the struggle for racial justice came about in the most unexpected, artistic way.

Twenty days had passed since America watched Philando Castile die. That afternoon, I decided to replace the anger bubbling in my stomach with actual food. I sat down to a plate of homemade chicken carbonara—my favorite—but just as I spun those creamy noodles and bits of bacon around my fork, I was transported into a sort of dream state.

I always feel awkward about sharing this story, because I'm quick to give woo-woo people the side-eye—and this story is very woo-woo. So if having a life-altering vision isn't your idea of a typical Monday afternoon, no worries, it's not mine either. It's weird, and it's okay for you to feel like it's weird.

It went something like this.

Walking by a park, I heard the faint roar of an impassioned street preacher. I've never liked street preachers, even less so after the racism I experienced from white Christians. Still, I followed his voice into the park until I was standing close enough to discover that the preacher was me.

Street-preacher Andre was standing next to a large, lumpy white boulder, and on that rock was inscribed a million racial injustices: housing discrimination, police brutality, the names of Black victims of police violence. I watched my preacher-self recite ancient Hebrew poetry, once sung centuries before by prophetic outcasts, about a world where tears are obsolete because the -isms and phobias that uphold society's routine violence have been abolished.

Then I came to—sitting in my living room, my tears diluting the carbonara sauce on my noodles.

I wept because I recognized that boulder immediately. It represented how heavy Blackness can be. In our bodies, we bear the trauma of our heroic, terrorized ancestors as we navigate a world where many still regard us with suspicion and contempt. Blackness can feel like an invisible burden we always have in tow.

I also wept because I felt the vision was an instruction, and I did not want to do it. When I said I'd commit my body to the struggle, I assumed I'd do so like a sane person, not by walking about with a pet rock everywhere I go. But I couldn't shake off the vision as some weird daydream and go on about my day. I feared I'd regret it if I refused to obey. Maybe I would feel guilty later, or I'd always wonder what would have happened if I had taken it seriously. So I decided I would do it.

Bang!

Clunk.

Bang!

I must have spent a full minute trying to find the right angle to get a bright green metal cart with a hundred-pound granite boulder on it through the door of my Greek class the next morning.

When I told myself I'd go through with that symbolic act, I kind of hoped that I'd find it impossible. Where was I going to find a boulder? How was I going to get it from place to place? But those details came together so easily, it almost felt like it was destined to happen.

"Where can I find a bulky, large boulder?" I asked Facebook.

At first, I got a bunch of unhelpful, witty responses. People suggested I drive to the beach or the desert to find one. I determined that if I had to drive ninety minutes to the beach or go traipsing into the wilderness for this thing, it probably wasn't meant to be. The universe knows I don't like driving or the outdoors and wouldn't ask me to do that. But just as I was about to say, "Well, Dre, you tried your best," and move on with my life, my phone chimed.

"How big?" read the text message. It was my classmate Aaron. I knew that if he was asking what size boulder I wanted, then he must have one. I didn't have a chance to respond before more messages rolled in.

Ding! He texted me a photo.

Ding! Another photo.

Ding!

Apparently, there were several daunting boulders lodged in his yard. I was speechless at how easily the boulder seemed to be turning up. He invited me over to peruse them. This took the "I don't know where to find the boulder" excuse off the table.

I crossed my fingers and asked where he lived. Usually, we Angelenos can justify flaking out on just about any commitment because we've got to drive too far to get there. Not this time. Aaron lived ten minutes away. Strike excuse number two.

My last hope to get out of it was to tell Aaron what I'd seen and what I felt compelled to do, in hopes he might say I sounded like a crazy person. Perhaps the people in my life would recognize that I had had some kind of nervous breakdown and tell me to drink more water and stop skipping meals. But when I arrived at his home and told him and his wife, Sarah, about the vision, they said, "Do you need us to buy you a wagon for your rock?" They prayed for me, offered their home anytime I needed to rest, and then Aaron walked me outside to help choose a boulder.

I imagined I'd pick a cartoonishly big rock, the kind you'd picture falling on Wile E. Coyote. There was just that sort of rock a few steps from the door—a tiny mountain. I set my shoulder against it, tightened my stomach, and pushed with a grunt. And for all the effort, my feet slid on the slick grass beneath me, but the rock hadn't moved an inch. "Yeah, that's solid granite," Aaron chuckled. "All of them are." They weren't going to move so easily. The boulder I would carry would look much smaller than I expected.

The one I ended up choosing was definitely large, about the size of my torso, but at first glance it seemed manageable. Looks were misleading, though. I needed Aaron's help to get it off the ground and into the trunk of my car. When we dropped it into the backseat, the entire car bounced under its weight. Aaron turned to me and asked, "When is your Sabbath?"

"Saturday," I answered.

"Okay. I'll come and get this from you on Saturday mornings, and I'll bring it back to you on Sunday afternoons."

And just like that, I was out of excuses. If I chose not to perform what I'd seen in the vision, I'd have to admit that it was because I just didn't want to. That boulder was all but handed to me on a platter.

That night, I painted that rock under a motion light by the door of my home music studio.

Bang!

Clunk!

The first day dragging that thing around was about as embarrassing as I'd feared. In Beginning Greek, the entire class watched as I tried to get it through the doorway, struggling like I was Charlie Chaplain. I kept my eyes to the floor to avoid seeing how many people noticed how odd I looked.

Once inside, I looked up and there was my friend Christian. "What's that, the white man's burden?" he said playfully.

"Kinda." I shrugged.

I scanned the room for somewhere to park the thing. Whoever designed that room—amphitheater-style seating with no ramps—clearly never expected a student would need to cart a boulder to his or her desk. All of the seats were behind long white desks on brown-carpeted steps that cascaded down to the floor. There was no way to get it up those steps, and the only place on the floor where it wouldn't have been a fire hazard was in the center of the room next to the teacher's projector station. So that's where I set it.

The professor asked, "Would you like to share with the class what this is about?"

"This boulder represents the burden that racism places on the Black psyche," I explained. I shared the effect of Philando Castile's death and others on many Black Americans.

The professor asked that the class take a moment and reflect on what I had shared in a moment of silence and spent the rest of the period hopping over that boulder to get to the whiteboard. Something seemed surprisingly appropriate about the whole scene: the thing much of America wants to ignore sitting in the center of the room, in full view of everyone. When class ended, one of the only other Black students in the room approached me. "Thank you," he said, then walked away.

After class, I carted the boulder to the center of campus and began to write all of the things I could remember from the vision on it with a black Sharpie—sometimes needing to trace over letters multiple times to make the words more legible. Then I sat next to it and sang whatever songs came to mind: Bob Marley's "Redemption Song," "We Shall Overcome," whatever freedom songs I knew.

Some administrators stopped by to sit and sing with me. Some students hurried by about their business. Other pedestrians grinned, moved in slowly, and threw change at my feet like I was busking on the Barcelona promenade.

In the months that followed, with the rock in tow, nearly every experience of mine was imbued with deeper meaning. One memory has never left me. I was attempting to unload the boulder from the car and place it on the cart. Because it was so dense, I'd developed a very specific technique for getting it out of the car. I would usually do a squat, then roll it into my arms and then let it roll onto the cart.

But this time, as it rolled into my arms, I lost my footing and slipped onto my back. I lay there, pinned to the ground for a moment, with the weight of it resting on my chest, immobilized on the cold ground of that parking garage with no help in sight.

One day I was lugging the boulder through the foyer of a campus building when I ran into a friend who'd seen me post about it on Facebook. We sighed together about Philando Castile's death and followed the flow of conversation to the connection between racial profiling and chattel slavery.

There was a little roofless kiosk in that lobby where campus safety officers sat throughout the day. Kevin, the close friend who had shared the article about the white father forgiving the police, was on duty that day. He overheard me and my friend talking and felt compelled to interrupt. He explained that many kinds of slavery have existed in the world throughout history— a common rebuttal from white people about slavery. I'm not sure if they think we don't know that slavery wasn't invented in America or that it somehow makes the *Maafa* less egregious, but they sure seem to love saying it.

I told Kevin that this wasn't a discussion about slavery as an abstract concept but about the specific legacy of a particular system of anti-Black violence affecting particular people—including me. "I can't categorically condemn slavery," he said, "because some slaves might have had a positive experience." He went on: some slaveowners were benevolent. For a moment, it sounded like he wouldn't have minded if the institution had never ended.

This was the most awkward way for me to find out someone I loved was a racist. The earlier conversation had been one thing, about the father who didn't get upset at the police, but I couldn't believe I was hearing Kevin defend chattel slavery—to my face!

This same Kevin once sat next to me as I lay on the floor of the seminary chapel in the dark, crying, "God *can't* be real." The very same Kevin once helped me arrange my travel plans and organize a deferment on my coursework when I found out one of my family members had died. Now he was looking me in the face telling me slavery wasn't such a bad idea. You mean to tell me this whole time, Kevin thought the idea of human bondage had potential? It made me question how he really saw us. All that support I got from him—was it a friend helping a friend, or did he consider himself a benevolent master?

I turned to my friend, the one Kevin had interrupted, and we just looked at each other in amazement. We both knew that some white Americans thought and spoke the way Kevin did. We just didn't expect someone in our seminary would have the gall to defend slavery to a Black person in mid-protest of anti-Black violence. We gave each other a look that said, "Abort conversation," shook hands, and agreed to talk later. Then we parted ways, leaving Kevin alone in his kiosk.

It took me a few days to reach out to Kevin and share my experience of that conversation. I was reluctant to bring it up, but I couldn't just hang out with him again without addressing that he'd basically said it wasn't that bad for my ancestors to be stolen, tortured, stigmatized, and subjugated. So, I wrote him a message. I told him that I felt betrayed by his defense of slavery. His response surprised me:

> I cannot invalidate the experiences and choices of large groups of people throughout history by flatly declaring them as categorically evil wether [sic] that be the decision to buy a slave or to remain a slave.
>
> I draw a distinction between the institution of slavery and the violation of human rights these can be mutually exclusive. And I believe they have been in some situations and households throughout history.

It's important to note that I didn't ask Kevin to explain his slavery comments. I expressed that his words had caused offense. But instead of seeking to heal our relationship, he spent the majority of his response rehashing his argument. He invited me to breakfast the next morning if I wanted to talk more.

That was the second time Kevin used the word "can't" in regard to condemning slavery: first in the seminary lobby, second in his message. That word choice is interesting to me. The fact that he'd doubled down on that language makes it feel more meaningful. He echoed his predecessors, who often wrote about how they *couldn't* abolish slavery, because the world they were building depended on it too much. A straight line can be traced between the colonizers who claimed they couldn't abolish slavery to white people today who "can't" condemn it in the present, nor imagine a world without its descendants: the police and prisons. Perhaps they do this because they know they can't categorically condemn the violence that structures their world without implicating themselves.

Kevin invited me to breakfast to talk it over the next morning. I couldn't accept the invitation. "I don't know, man," I said. "This changes things."

I haven't seen Kevin in person since the day he defended slavery in the lobby of Fuller Seminary. At first, I needed some time to process the fact that, even when confronted, my "good friend" obviously didn't think it a big deal to tell a Black man that chattel slavery might have been justifiable. I expected him to at least see that. The prospect of getting food the very next day and having to listen to him repeat that nonsense wasn't something I wanted to do.

I did eventually reach out to Kevin, arranging a time to talk over drinks. But somewhere between reaching out and the actual day we were supposed to hang, a Heineken commercial, of all things, changed my mind.

The company released an ad called "Worlds Apart" that made waves on the Internet. The four-minute commercial showed people who were "political opposites" having blind-date style conversations over a beer. They paired a climate change denier with an environmentalist, a self-proclaimed feminist with a male supremacist, a transgender woman and a transphobic cisgender man. Each pair spends some initial time getting acquainted and does a brief building project; then the pair is shown a video in which the two participants themselves present a more strident version of their views, highlighting their "differences." They're given a choice: leave the room, or chat over a beer. All of the pairs choose to talk. From the clips we see, all of the conversations seem to go well.

Americans seem to believe our lives should be like that Heineken ad. That if we can just get proximate to one another, close enough to really see and be seen, we can overcome our differences and live happily ever after.

While I agree that proximity has its merits, the commercial had the opposite effect on me than the company intended. The more I watched, the more I wondered: *Why should these representatives of persecuted minority groups have to sit down and convince someone else that their lived experiences are valid?* These were not just differences of perspective. Some of these people had been put in a position to defend their very existence. That's not fair.

Furthermore, watching those conversations play out made me realize that not all perspectives are valid or deserving of an audience. A transphobe is not entitled to tell a trans person that they're mentally ill. A misogynist doesn't deserve to sit down with a woman to tell her she should be subservient to men. And I wasn't about to sit down with some white man, no matter our history, and explain to him why it would be wrong for someone to hold me as their property. He should know that already. And if he's my friend, he should feel that already.

The problem of racial injustice isn't just that people have differing opinions but that some people are so dependent on anti-Black violence that they can't imagine the world without it, while others of us are actually Black. It's insulting to suggest that we should come together and debate over that.

Some people assume that we do need to debate with racists because they believe we need everyone on board to create change. That's incorrect. Social progress is often the work of a committed, creative minority. A massive study on nonviolent movements by sociologists Maria J. Stephan and Erica Chenoweth revealed that as little as 3.5 percent of a population in sustained nonviolent struggle has consistently proven to be enough to topple dictators and revolutionize a society.[6] If only I'd known about that study when I first got started.

In the early days of my awakening, I thought the world was split into two kinds of people: those deeply committed to racial hierarchy and those committed to fighting against it. I thought my job was to sit down with those committed to racial hierarchy and help them see the error of their ways. "Aren't you exactly the kind of person they need to be talking to?" people love to ask. "If you want to do something about racial injustice, you're going to have to persuade those who disagree with you." For years, I bought into that way of thinking. And while it's true that those who want to build a movement for racial justice will have to persuade some reluctant people to join, it's untrue that the work is primarily about converting staunch opponents into avid supporters.

I learned eventually that support for racial progress is a spectrum, not a binary. On one extreme are the leading Black freedom movement activists, like Patrisse Cullors, a co-founder of the Black Lives Matter movement. On the opposite extreme are active opposers, like the neo-Nazi leader Richard Spencer. But between those poles, an array of other attitudes toward the movement exists. There are folks who are opposed to the movement but not actively organizing to thwart it—we call them passive opposers. There are those who feel neutral on the issues the movement is fighting against. Then there are passive allies who say they're totally against racism but aren't actively doing anything to fight against it.

When I came to understand that there is a spectrum of allies for racial progress—not a binary—I realized that Black people don't have to sit down and discuss the validity of our struggle with people who don't think chattel slavery was all that bad an idea. Movement experts suggest that our best bet at mobilizing for social progress is to target the groups in the middle of the spectrum: activate the passive supporters and get the neutrals to care about the issue. Too often, we get bogged down in trying to convince active opposers to racial progress to agree with us. But we can change the world in spite of their opposition by focusing on people who are in the movable middle. Otherwise, we waste all of our energy deliberating with people like Kevin, who refuse to call slavery categorically wrong, much less fight white supremacy in the present day.

This notion of a spectrum of allies continues to be one of the most liberating truths about social change for me. It allows Black people to preserve our energy and tend to our mental health by avoiding dinner dates with people who are committed to our oppression. There's no need for Black people to wear ourselves out trying to drag racists kicking and screaming out of their anti-

Blackness. Let non-Black people figure out how to best appeal to hard-to-move non-Black people.[*] We'll focus on the people who are movable.

Around the time I decided against a dinner debate with Kevin, my friend Mackenzie invited me to perform in an artist showcase she was curating. The show was called "Listen LA," and featured various types of artists: spoken word, poetry, dance, and music. All of the artists were Black, performing work about racial justice.

I hadn't thought of lugging the boulder as a creative action until people in my social circle started pointing it out. The first was a seasoned community organizer backstage at one of my shows at a famous music venue, Hotel Café in Hollywood. When they saw me haul the boulder into the green room, they said, "I guess you're—like—an artivist now."

I felt like I'd just been knighted. Before then, I hadn't thought of myself as an activist, because I wasn't leading street protests or canvassing at the local grocery store. *But a bona fide Black Lives Matter activist called me an artivist,* I gasped. I was as honored as I was surprised that they acknowledged my artistic expressions as legitimate movement work. I took that label like an oversize, hand-me-down T-shirt I hoped to grow into one day.

---

[*] Non-Black people, if you're asking the question of how to appeal to passive opposers of racial justice, the work of my friend Greg Satell, author of *Cascades: How to Create a Movement That Drives Transformational Change,* may appeal to you. He suggests using the opposition's talking points to appeal to shared values. Kind of how Dr. King used America's democratic ideals to confront racism, as in: "You say you care about democracy? So do we! Racism isn't democratic."

My close friends also confirmed that I'd stumbled into the intersection of art and activism. They called my boulder protest "performance art." Again, I hadn't thought of it that way, but when they called it that, it felt like an epiphany. Though I'd been experiencing some sort of songwriter's block for over a year, I was still an artist at heart. I realized that I'd been responding to anti-Black violence with art for a while. From writing my song "Oppression" in sixth grade to dragging the boulder in the then-present.

I never did very much with most of those songs I wrote about social justice before then because they didn't seem like the ones most people wanted to hear. People wanted worship songs from me when I was involved in church, and people in clubs in New York and Los Angeles wanted sexy love songs—or so I was told. But "Listen LA" offered me a platform to sing about what it's like to inhabit a Black body. From that time forward, I began intentionally looking to music again as a way to process my feelings about my Black existence.

I'd invited Kevin to come to the show. If he came, I thought, it would give him a chance to learn about racism without requiring the labor of a one-on-one tutoring session—a win-win. Perhaps he could hear me best in my element, through music and performance and in the context of a cloud of witnesses.

The night for "Listen LA" came. Backstage, the cast marveled at the turnout. Hundreds of people had come to receive our performances, and most of the audience was white—people from the middle wedges of the spectrum of support. I listened in awe as my colleagues performed their work. They were so powerful, ruthless, compelling, and free in their artistic expressions. When my turn came, I decided to start my performance from the back of the room, slowly coming up the center aisle with my boulder in tow. I belted out two verses of Bob Dylan's "Blowin' in the Wind" as I approached the front, because I figured the mostly white crowd would recognize that song.

At the front, I turned to face the audience and went silent for a moment as I scanned the crowd for Kevin's face. I took my time. The silence grew just long enough to become dramatic, possibly awkward. But I didn't want to say a word until I saw my friend, my closest friend.

He wasn't there. I took a deep breath and began to tell the audience why I was lugging a boulder behind me.

6

We Can All Be White

One morning, I posted the cover art for that song I'd written in response to the killing of Eric Garner a couple years before. I was excited to finally have a song about racial justice that felt good enough to put out into the world. The graphic featured an American flag, the likeness of the U.S. Constitution with bullet holes in it, and protesters in gas masks. By then, I'd lost enough friends for posting about racism to expect some pushback. "I just watched the lyric video we're going to put out for this song and thought about all the people who are going to unfriend me :)," I posted to Facebook.

"Minnesota cop is a Latino, not white," a white former college classmate responded. He was referring to Philando Castile's killer, though I had only posted the artwork for my song with no mention of specific police violence victims. "Just sayin' not justifying what happened, just pointing out that it's not always a white cop."

Another white friend commented, "So if when a black person kills another black person it is a product of white supremacy, then when a white person kills another white person it's?"

"It's always white supremacy," the first commenter quipped. And for a moment the two scoffing commenters seemed thick as thieves.

Never mind that they were completely off-topic. The scoffing white guys failed to understand something crucial about anti-Blackness, as many people do: that nonwhite people of color can, and often do, perpetuate anti-Blackness—the apocalyptic lesson I'll unpack in this chapter.

I responded to their comments with an analogy about slavery, to explain that one's complexion doesn't prevent them from participating in anti-Black violence. Just because slaveholders sometimes used Black men as slave drivers to keep their other Black captives in line and working, this didn't mean that slavery wasn't about white supremacy. The Black slave driver was a slave enforcing the slave system, a victim of anti-Black violence and racial hierarchy enforcing racial hierarchy through anti-Black violence. The melanin content in his skin wasn't some magical compound that prevented him from lifting a hand against his kinfolk. His so-called owner was likely to reward him with better treatment—double portions of food, better housing, and gifts, for instance—and special privileges to secure his loyalty.[1] In that way, slaveholders tried to divide the oppressed population and weaken the possibility of uprisings.

My white friends didn't respond to this explanation. I did, however, get a private message from another former college classmate, a Puerto Rican woman named Gina, that proved the exact point I was making that day and in this chapter.

"You should check yourself," she wrote.

"Did you mean to send that message to me?" I asked

"Yes," she replied. Then she began to lecture me about how I'd been posting "hateful" things about white people.

I was a bit surprised that Gina came at me like that, because I hadn't yet understood that non-Black people of color are not automatically our allies. She and I had been pen pals for about two years by then. We had each other's phone numbers. If we were friends, and she was concerned that my actions were misguided, a phone call and conversation would've been possible and appropriate—not a reprimand.

I shook my head at her message. She wasn't white. So why, I wondered, did she feel so offended by me calling out white people's racist behavior? And she reprimanded me with just as much energy as any white person in those days.

In hindsight, Gina's reaction sticks out as one of many examples from my personal life of how anti-Blackness compels people of color to align with white people and the challenge that presents for building multiracial coalitions for racial progress. In the wake of Philando Castile's death, I encountered several Latino former college classmates eager to defend white people and denigrate Black people. Any time I spoke up about how white people perpetuate white supremacy, they were some of the most ardent people to jump in and reprimand me. And from those encounters came the uncomfortable apocalyptic lesson I alluded to above.

In a 2018 lecture entitled "Can 'White' People Be Saved," Yale professor Willie James Jennings was explaining how the fusion of white identity and Christianity had been an essential part of the evolution of patriarchy, racism, and the climate crisis, when he liberated himself from his notes for a moment. "Anyone can be white, friends," he declared in a moment of spontaneous inspiration.[2] In the recording, the energy in the lecture hall feels more like a Baptist church, with yelps, claps, and hoots shooting through the auditorium. "If you've not followed this so far, let me be clear," he continued, "no one is born white. There's no white biology." Whiteness, he explained, is a way of thinking and being in the world.

Whiteness includes the logic of human hierarchy based on race, gender, sexuality, ability, wealth, and religion that has been used for centuries to justify economic inequality and oppressive politics. The people we call "white" occupy the top of that hierarchy, as humanity's ideal and standard form.

I'll never forget having a conversation about police brutality over Shake Shack burgers with a white woman friend who said, "If they just dressed normally, maybe that wouldn't have happened to them." I pressed her to tell me what she imagined "normal" people look like. After several attempts, she eventually confessed: "I guess . . . they look like me." Her eyes opened wide, cheeks turned red, as she grabbed her mouth in shock. But "white people" aren't the only folks who think like this. All people in white societies are trained to see the world through the lens of whiteness, regardless of complexion.

In this climate, nonwhite people often end up thinking of white people as default humans. And when we do, whiteness becomes the standard we strive toward. Many of us judge each other by how well we assimilate. When immigrants of color poke fun at each other's accents when speaking English, they're measuring how well other nonwhite people speak a European language. The standard of whiteness is why Black women are among the least right-swiped profiles on Tinder, and why some Black kids tease their eloquent friends for "sounding white." If we're not careful, we easily fall into the trap of appraising each other by how well we can perform whiteness.

In many ways, the white world demands that all people be as white as they can. But while many are called, few are chosen. Some people will never be mistaken for white people, but they still try their best to assimilate. Some people straighten or dye their hair or name their children a common white name. Others earn advanced degrees from predominantly white institutions or marry a white person. But the most accessible way to try to climb the ranks of human hierarchy, to ascend into whiteness, is anti-Black violence.

As I've mentioned before, the line between white people and other races has always been drawn in blood. Hunting indigenous people, burning African captives, beating Black patrons on segregated busses, lynching Black people, kicking in doors and roughing up citizens in drug searches, and constant viral police killings—all of that violence reaffirms who stands where in the racial hierarchy. And although non-Black people of color are fellow victims of white supremacy, they often participate in anti-Blackness as they seek to assimilate into white society.

In race conversations, I've often heard non-Black people of color complain about a Black/white binary that crowds out their racial suffering and freedom efforts. They may be right that some people think only in terms of Black and white when talking about race. However, non-Black people of color may not be as overlooked by Black people as they think. In many cases, they aren't mentioned in these conversations because many Black people have experienced enough anti-Blackness from non-Black people of color that we think of them as white people's accomplices—we take that as a given.

Granted, there are many examples of solidarity between Black people and non-Black people of color. Lifelong Asian American activist Grace Lee Boggs was highly active in the Black Power movement of the 1960s and pioneered more multiracial revolutionary organizations than I have room to name here. Activist Yuri Kochiyama,* who pushed for reparations to Japanese Americans for their internment in the U.S. during World War II, was a member of the Pan-Africanist group the Organization of Afro-American Unity founded by Malcolm X; she held Brother Malcolm in her arms as he breathed his last in the Audubon Ballroom. In 1969, Chicago Black Panther Party chairman Fred Hampton brought together two Chicano groups (the Brown Berets and the Young Lords), activists from the American Indian Movement, and a Chinese American group called the Red Guard Party to fight for social progress in Chicago.

At the same time, non-Black communities of color have also been channels for anti-Black violence. As my prophetic namesake André 3000 once pointed out: all over the world, darker-skinned people are treated with contempt by those more

---

* Seems like a good time to note that I know that throughout this book I quote and mention freedom fighters who were *not* committed to nonviolent struggle. This is because we still have something to learn from people with whom we share fundamental disagreements.

proximate to whiteness. This fact is clearly seen in the ethnic cleansing and population whitening projects of some South American countries, the massacres of Australia's aboriginal people, and the persecution of darker-skinned people in some parts of the Caribbean and Asia. Black people don't just experience anti-Blackness from white people; we experience it from all kinds of cultures. I've seen this dynamic up close.

When I was in college, I fell in love with a beautiful Peruvian woman. When she told her parents I was Black, they asked her if she was going through "a rebellious phase" and refused to take the relationship seriously.

When I moved into an apartment in a mostly Chinese neighborhood in Los Angeles, it took months for my neighbors—most of them of Asian descent—to accept that a Black man was living in their apartment complex. "Where are you going?" a tenant asked me after seeing me use my key to unlock the front gate. A different tenant asked me the same question on another occasion after seeing me going up the steps to my apartment. Yet another afternoon, my key wasn't working so well. A neighbor stood at the gate and watched me jiggle the lock for a good minute, refusing to help. Meanwhile, whenever my Chinese American girlfriend came over to hang out, she would slip in and out of the complex without a problem. People opened the door for her, even though they'd never seen her before or seen us together!

I know many Black people who share experiences like the ones I've recounted. It's common to hear about clerks at the bodega or beauty supply watching Black patrons more closely, and in many of these stories, the shopkeeper is more likely to be Indian, Korean, or North African than white. Remember the story I told earlier, about the landlord who refused to rent to me in Harlem when he saw what I look like? He was Asian American. These stories, and countless others, have taught Black people that it's common for nonwhite people to view us through the anti-Black lenses of the white world.

In her book *Why Are All the Black Kids Sitting Together in the Cafeteria? And Other Conversations About Race,* Dr. Beverly Tatum analogizes anti-Blackness to a smog.[3] The smog has messed up the air quality for everyone. We've all inhaled it, which means everyone's lungs have been affected. Since everyone's breathed it in, everyone exhales it too. We are all smog breathers, Tatum says.

Even Black people are smog breathers. Bill Cosby's famous 2004 "Pound Cake" speech, where he stereotypes Black slang and refers to Black people as "these people," comes to mind, as do the self-hating diatribes of conservative darling Candace Owens, who regularly gaslighted Black Lives Matter protesters by calling them "whiny toddlers pretending to be oppressed."[4] I've encountered the latter kind of Black anti-Blackness myself.

One morning I posted on Facebook, "Black boys deserve to grow up," in response to another viral police killing. There have been so many that I can't even remember which one was killed that time. But I do remember how a former classmate, a Black man, came out of the woodwork denigrating Black youth as "savages who need to be shipped off to an island somewhere." He stopped short of outright calling Black youth superpredators, as criminologists once described us in the 1990s. But that was the flavor of his rhetoric.

When Black people talk like that, it doesn't signal that race isn't a factor in Black suffering. It signals the success of the project of white supremacy. White supremacy has always been on the lookout for Black spokespeople, because a domination system will operate more smoothly when the subjugated comply. Patriarchy is at peace when women "know their place." Homophobia is at peace when lesbian, bisexual, and gay people stay in the closet. Slavery is at peace when the enslaved are "well-behaved." Which is why the holy grail of oppression is to convert victims into spokespeople. If Black people can inhale and exhale the smog of this anti-Black world, anyone can. We can all (try to) be white.

So, yes. A Latino cop, regardless of his personal feelings, can enact white supremacy by performing a job that was created by white supremacists to preserve and reinforce the racial hierarchy. And a Puerto Rican woman like Gina can perform whiteness by trying to silence the protests of Black people against white supremacy.

The prevalence of anti-Black assumptions and behavior among nonwhite people raises important questions about building interracial coalitions for racial progress. Coalitions are an essential part of pursuing social change through nonviolent struggle because any group large enough to demand change is likely to include people of diverse backgrounds. Serbian revolutionary Srdja Popovic notes that "a revolution only picks up steam when two or more groups that have nothing to do with one another decide to join together for their mutual benefit."[5] Bridges will always have to be built, whether across ideologies or social identities like race, gender, ability, age, sexuality, and class.

The apocalyptic lesson of this chapter—that anti-Blackness is everywhere—brings nuance to the revolutionary principle of the last chapter—that there's a spectrum of allies, that our best bet is to search for them in the movable middle. But how do we identify those allies in the first place? Clearly, complexion and ethnicity can't be the only factors.

Since anti-Blackness is a known problem in communities of color, should we forget about building bridges across race and look for allies within Blackness exclusively? And if anti-Blackness is a problem among Black people, then where does that leave us? Black-led racial justice groups must answer these questions according to their specific values and contexts.

It's legitimate for individual Black-led racial justice groups to work exclusively with Black people. In theory, it's possible for Black people to build a viable all-Black, nonviolent movement for racial progress and win. At 13 percent of the U.S. population, Black people have around four times the numbers that have been needed to topple dictators and defeat empires around the world—this fact can be liberating for Black folks who don't want to deal with the anti-Black nonsense of non-Black people of color. We don't have to. Black people can liberate ourselves by ourselves, and all people would benefit, because all the systems of oppression we face today intersect in Blackness, which means they would all have to unravel to make Black people free.

At the same time, there's a valid argument to be made for interracial coalitions in the struggle for racial progress. Though non-Black allies aren't needed in the struggle for Black liberation, that doesn't mean they're never welcome. History has already proven that anti-Blackness in communities of color doesn't make interracial collaboration impossible. The abolition movement against slavery involved white conductors on the Underground Railroad and Mexican sympathizers who provided refuge to Black fugitives. The Civil Rights Movement enlisted white clergy and students to join in their demonstrations—some to the point of suffering violence or death. And I witnessed, firsthand, majority-Asian communities holding Black Lives Matter rallies to address anti-Blackness in their communities in L.A. in the summer of 2020. There have always been non-Black accomplices in the fight for Black freedom, and there will continue to be in the future.

Black people and non-Black people of color also have a common enemy in American imperialism, which has used the violence of economic exploitation, oppressive politics, war, and colonization against us. Therefore, the end of white supremacy is a place where the interests of many diverse groups converge. For these reasons, collaboration across race seems to be the most realistic scenario for making racial progress.

Remember: oppressive systems often use a divide-and-conquer strategy to keep oppressed communities from banding together in common struggle. At the risk of being reductive about it, racism is one of those strategies. The violent, male-dominated, white supremacist, profit-driven, plunderous, expansionist, oppressive system we live under wants to convince the people they subjugate that we are each other's enemies. And they've been successful for ages.

Consider how Virginia's colonial elites consolidated racial caste after white indentured servants and oppressed Africans joined forces to oppose Governor William Berkeley in 1675. The authorities passed the Virginia Slave Codes of 1705 to keep the races separate and to prevent future multiracial uprisings.*

Consider how long middle-class and poor white Americans have been the foot soldiers of the very same system that exploits their labor, on the basis that Black people are out to assault their women and that immigrants are coming for their jobs.

The reason those who benefit most from the white supremacist system have reacted so strongly to multiracial collaboration is because they know solidarity makes us strong. That's why Fred Hampton once said so confidently, "We don't think you fight fire with fire best; we think you fight fire with water best. We're not gonna fight racism with racism, but we're gonna fight it with solidarity."[6]

But solidarity is complicated. Solidarity can't mean we all just put our differences aside. It will mean working through our differences and doing internal work to unlearn anti-Blackness. Non-Black people of color will have to acknowledge the way anti-Blackness appears in their communities and find practical ways to address it. They'll have to learn to talk about racial oppression in ways that don't erase the nuance between the struggle of people of color against white supremacy, nor Black people's struggle against anti-Blackness.

On the other hand, Black people who choose to work with non-Black people will have to be careful not to essentialize non-Black people as irredeemable. It will take patience with non-

---

* I'm referring to Bacon's Rebellion, and since I am, I have to acknowledge that Nathaniel Bacon seemed to be driven by anti-Indigenous sentiment. I think the point about the power of cross-racial coalitions is still relevant, but it also bears saying that Bacon's Rebellion is complicated.

Black colleagues of color as they unlearn some of the prejudices and habits they learned from mainstream society.

This brings me to a tenet of principled nonviolent struggle that may be useful to Black people collaborating with non-Black people who are unlearning anti-Blackness: that nonviolent revolutions target systems of oppression, not people. Dr. King wrote, "The attack is directed against forces of evil rather than against persons who happen to be doing the evil."[7] This principle can help us choose the right targets for our attack on racial oppression. The target is the system of white supremacy itself, not individuals who appear to be white. The targets of our revolution are the resources of power—political, social, and economic—that make it possible for that system to operate, not your white friend-of-a-friend Trevor.

This question of interracial coalitions is all the more important as the white backlash to racial progress grows more openly fascist. The word *fascist* has been flying around more often since Donald Trump ran for president in 2015. And this is a good place to examine some of its meanings, because they relate directly to the idea of diverse coalitions. The most relevant fact about fascism, to the point of this chapter, is its origin story as a word. *Fascism* comes from a Latin term, *fasces,* that means "bundle of sticks." It evokes the image of a bunch of wood fastened together and attached to an ax-head; the term was used in Italian politics in the early twentieth century to describe the banding together of similar political factions. The basic idea in that word-image is that there's strength in same-group unity.

One might ask how I can identify same-group unity among Black people as a viable strategy for liberation but call same-group unity for white people fascist. The short answer to that rebuttal is that fascist coalitions coalesce to dominate, not to liberate.

Fascism begins with hysterical language about the dangers of racial progress and demographic change. When British protesters threw the statue of colonizer Edward Colston into a harbor in Bristol, England, in the summer of 2020, British journalist Melanie Phillips wrote, "They are accusing the police and white society of being fundamentally evil . . . these demonstrations have been a form of insurrection against western society and its institutions." Note how she said the quiet part out loud by using "white society" and "western society" all but interchangeably.[8] In the spring of 2021, Tucker Carlson warned his millions of viewers, "Demographic change is the key to the Democratic Party's political ambitions. They're no longer trying to win you over with their program. They're obviously not trying to improve your life. They don't even really care about your vote anymore. Their goal is to make you irrelevant."[9]

White people bundle together in fearful response to these omens of their alleged imminent irrelevance. We saw this bundling most obviously as almost all of the U.S. map turned GOP-red for Donald Trump on election night 2016, a direct response to the eight years of America's first Black president. We saw it again in Charlottesville when hundreds of tiki torch–wielding white men bundled together to announce, "Jews will not replace us!" And once again, as they bundled together to attack the U.S. Capitol in an attempt to stop Joe Biden from becoming president in 2021.

If we take Fred Hampton's strategy—to fight fire with water—

seriously, then we must consider that their racially homogeneous unity to consolidate power is probably best opposed by a racially diverse coalition that seeks an equitable distribution of power. A common side effect of nonviolent struggle supports my suggestion here: that the skills people must develop to organize effective nonviolent movements are similar to the skills they need in a healthy democratic society, because both involve the mass participation of diverse groups.[10] On that basis, pursuing racial justice through nonviolent struggle, in racially diverse coalitions, would challenge us to practice the same skills in the present that are necessary to live in the world we plan to build in the future. The divide-and-conquer strategy of this death-dealing system may be best confronted through a united front. To confront white supremacy, we'll all have to overcome the lies whiteness has told us to keep us separate.

7

Breaking Up with White Jesus

awoke that morning and dressed for a funeral, though to my knowledge no one had died. I'd had a dream weeks before where I saw myself dressed in a black suit, holding white lilies, as though I were at a graveside service. Blood spattered on the flowers, and the names of Black victims of police violence were written in white all over my suit jacket. Like the earlier vision with the boulder, the image of me in funeral clothes felt like an instruction.

Once I awoke in the real world again, I took a deep breath and imagined the jokes and comments I might encounter if I chose to perform what I'd seen. "Why do you want me to upset these people?" I sighed, not even sure to whom I was praying. God was feeling less real by the day, with every viral hashtag of another police victim. I wasn't excited about attracting more negative attention to myself by doing another performance protest, but the message of the performance convinced me to go through with it.

The vision invited me to go about in public mourning over people this society tells us aren't worth our grief. That message was too important to be censored by fear. So I took my only suit jacket and began to write the names of as many victims of police brutality as I could find on it with a white paint pen. On the back, I wrote in large letters "Stop killing us!" But unlike with the boulder, I didn't don the jacket immediately after writing on it. I waited.

On the morning of September 30, 2016, the word *today* flashed through my mind just as I was about to get dressed. It was time to put on the suit. Little did I know that in the wee hours of that morning, while I'd been sleeping, my neighbor Reginald "J.R." Thomas had been beaten to death by six Pasadena Police officers.

I didn't know J.R. personally. But his friends and family described him as an amicable guy, a father to eight children, who always walked around with his Bible in hand. He was also known to be living with mental illness.

The word on the street was that J.R. called 911 for help, and when police arrived on the scene, J.R. had a knife under one arm and a fire extinguisher in the other hand. Officers tased him, bound him, beat him with batons, and punched and kicked him until he died.

Hundreds of protesters filled the streets of Pasadena that night. They marched a four-mile circuit, from J.R.'s block down to Old Pasadena and back to his front door, blocking traffic and chanting his name along the way. Since I'd been doing so much in response to national stories of police brutality, I felt I had to be in the streets now that it'd happened in my own backyard. So, I joined the crowd once they returned to the neighborhood.

That night, I stood in the place where J.R. was killed, dressed in my funeral clothes.

Around that time, I'd picked up some gigs playing piano and singing at a few evangelical churches in the Los Angeles area. The pay wasn't great, but sometimes it made the difference between rationing leftover pizza for the week and actually going to the grocery store. By then, my faith had changed so much that sitting through sermons was too frustrating to endure, because preachers weren't speaking to any of my most pressing questions and concerns. I'd do the job onstage and wait in the lobby for the check. But on Sunday evenings, I'd still go to a local young adults' service with my roommates and suffer through the sermons there, for the sake of community.

The weekend after J.R.'s death, I was scheduled to lead the music at a Presbyterian church in a largely white suburb. I didn't feel like going, because I knew chances were slim that anything said or done in that service would have any relevance to the grief about racial violence I was holding. I'd been there through the wake of numerous Black deaths that triggered waves of outrage around the nation, but not a noticeable ripple in that sanctuary. I never heard a sermon that offered hope to Black people in light of the routine violence we navigate every day, not even a prayer for the families of police brutality victims. So I wasn't surprised at how the parishioners responded to the sight of my boulder and funeral suit bearing the names.

From the 7 A.M. soundcheck to the end of the second morning service at 12:15 P.M., no one said a word about the boulder and suit. The way people passed by without a word, you'd have thought every parishioner had lugged their own hundred-pound boulders to worship or worn a whole bunch of hashtags all over their jackets every Sunday.

Only one person made any comment that day. As I was leaving the sanctuary, I heard a voice call after me. "Hmm. Stop killing us," he read aloud, as though asking a question. I turned to see the man who read the message on my back. Then he chuckled, "Killing us with laughter, right?"

Jesus says somewhere in the Bible that all we need is a mustard seed of faith, which is just a speck. Tiny faith was all I had left by the time I was walking about in my funeral clothes. And I just knew that faith could grow, if God gave me a sign: like—oh! I don't know!—a faith-based mass movement for racial justice, as some Black churches had organized during the Civil Rights era. But white supremacy in the church sent my faith reeling to the floor. By the end of that year, I'd conclude that white Jesus was standing in the way of the revolution, and that realization made me seriously wrestle with questions about the role that spirituality, religion, and the divine have in the revolution for racial justice.

Beyond my personal hopes, I thought there were several reasons Christians should've been first in line to stand against racism. For one, the Christian religion is deeply implicated in the *Maafa* and the global system of racism that exists today. Popes issued papal bulls that gave colonizers permission to genocide indigenous people and take their lands.[1] Slaveholders quoted the New Testament—"slaves obey your masters"—at their captives. The first Klansmen to light a cross atop Stone Mountain built an altar there to "the Invisible Empire" and laid a sword, an American flag, and Holy Bible on it.[2] So, racism is, in large part, Christianity's mess to clean up.

Making all of this more urgent is the fact that Christian theology remains a formidable pillar of support for white supremacy today. White Christians—Protestant, Catholic, and Evangelical—played a large part in bringing Donald Trump into the Oval Office, throwing their support behind a man who ran on a racist platform. When it seemed clear that Trump would lose the 2020 election, well-known white, charismatic Christians begged God—or in the case of one viral video, "African angels"— to intervene.[3] And when insurrectionists attacked the U.S. Capitol in January 2021, many of them did so with the so-called Christian flag waving above their heads. We must take facts like these seriously. They tell us that many Christian institutions continue to shape and uphold a white supremacist common sense that makes the world hostile to Black people and makes white people willing to do dangerous things to preserve white power.

Some institutions shape and uphold that common sense directly and overtly, like the six Southern Baptist seminary presidents who wrote a statement denouncing Critical Race Theory as "incompatible with the gospel" (an echo of when Trump called antiracism education "anti-American").[4] Other Christian institutions reinforce our anti-Black common sense indirectly, like the many megachurches who refuse to preach about social justice for fear of upsetting conservative donors.

Although Christianity is in decline in the United States, 65 percent of Americans identified themselves as Christian in 2019, according to the Pew Research Center.[5] And Christianity is growing rapidly in South America, Africa, and Asia. This means two things. First, there can be no serious reckoning with global racism without giving serious attention to the ways Christianity continues to uphold white supremacy. Second: waiting for the colonizers' version of Christianity to just die off would be a mistake. Even as a minority social bloc, white Christians were able to install a white racist into one of the highest political offices in the world. And although there are many types of Christianity in the world, theologies passed down from slaveholders and colonizers are still being exported around the world through wildly popular evangelical ministry brands.

In the early years of the Black Lives Matter era, white Christianity's complicity in global racism, its enduring influence in culture, and its tremendous resources that could be mobilized for change were all reasons some Black people like myself held so much hope that they'd join the movement for Black lives. Instead, they gave us silence, spiritualized excuses, and now, in many cases, bad-faith opposition.

In a 2016 interview, seminary president and megachurch pastor John MacArthur was asked how Christians should engage the Black Lives Matter movement. MacArthur's response: "The object of life is no longer to fix past injustices. The object of life now is to proclaim Christ . . . once [people] come to Christ, all other issues fall away." He ties a bow around his white nonsense by adding, "When the gospel changes your life, you go from social issues to spiritual issues."[6]

Back then, I heard this notion—that social issues and spiritual issues are mutually exclusive—from so many white Christian leaders. From my former classmates who went on to become pastors to some of the most influential Christian leaders in the world, people were quick to find theological grounds for opposing the movement:

"Only Jesus can fix racism."

"In Christ we're all one."

"I don't believe in communal sin."

"We need to worry about biblical justice, not social justice."

"The Bible says submit to the authorities."

"Jesus never led a protest against Rome."

Around that time, a Facebook friend invited me to lunch with some folks from one of the largest and most influential Evangelical church networks in the world. The group was made up almost entirely of young Black and brown worshippers, frustrated that the church leadership wasn't speaking to the things that caused them anxiety from day to day: I.C.E. banging on their doors, police shooting people like them in traffic stops. They'd tried meeting with the pastor to convey to him what the church's silence meant to them. But these conversations had little effect on the preaching and prayers offered from the pulpit.

I graduated from Fuller Seminary around that time. I thought maybe I could put my tiny faith to work as a teaching pastor—perhaps I could be the change I want to see in the world and help Christians connect the dots between their faith and social justice. One of the largest Evangelical churches in America was looking to fill a couple of positions, and a longtime friend put me in touch. Around the third interview, one of the interviewers asked what I'd been up to lately. I told him about the boulder. From that point on, my artivism became a disproportionate focus of the interviews. "We all have issues that we care about," one interviewer said, "but we just want to keep the main thing the main thing, which is Jesus." Another leader explained, "Well, Andre, we're a large church, and the way we stay large is by avoiding conversations that might offend people."

By the time Keith Lamont Scott was fatally shot by a Black Charlotte police officer that September, I had lost all patience with Christian leaders telling me that silence about racism was spiritually correct. Days after Scott's death, the police released bodycam footage along with a statement. Officers thought they saw Scott rolling a joint—and later, holding a gun in his car. They said Scott exited the car with the firearm in his hand and backed away, failing to respond to repeated instructions to put it down.

The bodycam footage shows Mr. Scott standing by his vehicle with his arms at his sides. It's hard to tell whether or not there's a gun in his hand—it looks like he's just standing there.[7] Regardless, we know of several white men who've pointed guns at the police and survived. A white man aims a gun at police, and there's a standoff; a Black man holds anything that can be mistaken for a gun, and there's going to be another Black Lives Matter march. That's because in the minds of too many officers, a Black man with a gun is twice armed.

I remember watching eyewitnesses post videos to Twitter on the day of the killing, telling the world they had seen things that contradicted the police narrative. Remembering the year before, when South Carolina police were captured on video planting a weapon on Walter Scott, whom they'd shot in the back, I was partial to the testimonies of civilian eyewitnesses.

As I watched yet another wave of outrage erupt throughout Black America, my head filled with the sanctimonious excuses Christians used to justify their silence. I gave full vent to my frustration in a Facebook post as long as a CVS receipt. "Do I need to start tagging people?" I asked. I challenged the white evangelical pastors who'd criticized me for all the times I publicly expressed hope for divine intervention against anti-Black violence. Since they disagreed, I challenged them to say whatever it is they think Christians are supposed to say in the wake of a tragic event like Mr. Scott's death. No one answered.

A week later, I received a direct message on Facebook from a former classmate we'll call Hunter. Hunter and I were students in the same undergrad program in theology. After graduation, he went on to become the lead pastor of a church in small-town Florida. I hadn't heard from him or seen him since we sat in class over a decade earlier.

"Hey Andre, how's things?" he began.

I was a little leery about him reaching out so randomly, but I gave him the benefit of the doubt. "Hey man. I'm ok. How are you?"

He said he'd been doing all right, paused for a moment, then decided to cut the small talk: "Simply put, I believe you are abandoning the Gospel and church teaching in general in favor of the fashionable philosophies of our age, at least the beliefs which are fashionable in one particular political tribe. Specifically, it seems to me that you have all but abandoned any attempt at living out the second of the great commandments, to love your neighbor . . ."

I took a beat, then sent him my number and asked him to call me, because I thought a debate over the state of one's soul deserves better than a Facebook messenger conversation. He said he didn't have time to talk. It turns out he was just casually dropping by to tell me I'd broken the greatest commandment.

"What did you think would be the outcome of this exchange?" I asked. Did he expect I'd melt into tears and say he was right—*I repent! How hateful of me to say America needs to do something about racism!*—after which he could lead me in a repeat-after-me prayer to save my wretched soul?

"Ideally a phone call and a frank discussion," he replied. "But ultimately I hoped you could be made to see the problems with some of your ethical formulations."

At first, I basically told him to get lost. But about a week later, I wondered if I'd been too harsh. *Maybe Hunter was reaching out in good faith,* I thought, *even if he came off as presumptuous and arrogant. He deserved a fair chance.* So I circled back and asked him if he'd still like to talk. He did. We arranged a time for a video chat.

On the call, Hunter assumed the same posture of superiority as he had when he wrote to me on Facebook. I asked him what was so heretical about me saying that racism is a solvable problem that Christians should be first in line to confront. "It goes against the historic teachings of the church," he complained.

But there's a problem with that argument. If one only counts the teachings of slave-holding white theologians of early America as "historic church teaching"—Jonathan Edwards and George Whitefield, for example—then it logically follows that racial justice would have no part in their theology.

I asked Hunter why the teachings of Christian activists like Dr. Martin Luther King Jr. didn't count as historic church teachings. He refused to answer, and instead pivoted. "You don't sound like Dr. King," he said. "You sound like Malcolm X." That was supposed to be a dig at me—whitespeak for "Bad Negro."

When he made the Malcolm X comment, it was as though he'd banged a gavel. He sat back and looked into the camera trying to fight back a smirk. That was the sickest part of that exchange. He wasn't there to understand where I was coming from or even to defend "the Gospel," like he claimed. He'd come to shut me down and was just looking for the right line of rhetorical attack. He'd seen from my posts at the time that I had hope for divine intervention, and he was compelled to crush it.

When I asked him again why the notion that Christians should be eager to fight racism was so controversial, Hunter looked me in the eye and said, "Racism is not a priority to God."

I was stunned. Not that he'd said the words but at how naturally they came from his lips: like someone reading the time or telling you today's forecast. To my amazement, Hunter didn't seem to think he'd said anything incendiary. He seemed to think he spoke the truth plain and simple. And with that racist remark, I bid Hunter farewell. But I've never been able to forget what he'd said.

A few weeks later, I was supposed to play the piano at the Presbyterian church again. To get there on time, I needed to have left fifteen minutes earlier, but I was pinned to my living room couch by a question: "What if Hunter is right?"

I don't think they always realize this, but when a Christian says God isn't concerned about racism, they're saying God

doesn't care about Black people. Those statements are insepa-
rable. We fight for people we care about, period. If you saw a
friend in danger, love would compel you to try to save them. So
to say God won't intervene against anti-Black violence, because
it's not important, could only mean God doesn't love us. Hunter
had been more explicit than most in saying God didn't care
about racism, but his words helped me make sense of why so
many churches were silent about the movement for Black lives
at the time.

Had I dedicated my entire life to a God who doesn't love
Black people? The thought flooded the room, lifting the furni-
ture. I considered how the people who kidnapped and enslaved
my ancestors did so in Jesus's name; how they named one of
the first slave ships "Jesus";[8] how segregationists claimed racial
apartheid was God-ordained; how the descendants of those
Christian white supremacists were now telling me that divine
intervention was for whites only. I sank into deep waters of
doubt, the words of James Baldwin floating by: "God . . . is white.
And if His love was so great, and if He loved all His children,
why were we, the blacks, cast down so far?"

My whole life up to then, I'd defended Christianity against
the epithet that it was the "white man's religion." But that morning a terrifying epiphany washed over me: Didn't I once live as
though my Blackness wasn't important—as though Black rage
was inappropriate? And wasn't it white Christians who trained
me to live that way, keeping me in line by conflating love for God
with keeping white people comfortable? How many Black people throughout history had been kept in line like this, convinced
by slaveholder theology not to revolt against their oppressors?

Even Frederick Douglass once confessed that he had feared the wrath of God would follow him if he tried to run away from his so-called master.[9]

What if Christianity is for white people? I asked myself. *What if they made up this religion to serve their interests?* The thought made me tremble, but it made so much sense in that moment. All my life, I'd assumed God fought on the side of the oppressed. But that morning, it felt like God hadn't. God didn't prevent the slave ships from sailing, or the crosses from burning, or the bullets from piercing our bodies. "God is white," I whispered to myself again and again.

As it became clearer to me that their God was the divine sponsor of the *Maafa*, it became clear to me that white Jesus—as he'd been described in every church I attended—was also a white friend I couldn't keep. That was one of the most painful revelations of this apocalypse. My heart broke for a moment, feeling as though everything I'd believed in up to then had been a lie. I watched my concept of God die on my living room floor.

But moments later, the Jewish story of the Exodus came to mind. In that story, the Hebrew Bible depicts God emancipating the Israelites from slavery in Egypt. Clearly, the white friends I couldn't keep weren't singing to that God on Sunday mornings. That distinction was enough to get me to show up and play the piano that morning. For a while, I thought of God as the God of the Ghetto, who intervenes against systemic oppression. It was enough to keep me holding on to faith, but it couldn't keep me in church, because if the God of the Ghetto was real, They certainly weren't welcome there. There isn't room for me to unpack in detail how I discovered that, and where my spiritual journey went from there. Suffice to say that from then on, I started spending Sunday mornings at my favorite brunch spot rather than in church.

I didn't just reject Christianity when I left the church. I dismissed all spirituality as a distraction from the struggle for racial justice. That's because my encounters with white, nonreligious spiritual people didn't signal that they were much different from white Christians. They, too, were prone to the spiritual bypassing and victim blaming I'd witnessed in church. The only difference was one group said "God," and the other group said "the Universe."

I decided to let the pastors and gurus ponder the metaphysical while I looked for practical ways to interrupt systemic racism. For a while I considered myself a materialist, only interested in that which is tangible and verifiable through history and the senses. I accepted that the divine cavalry wasn't coming to help Black people, so we'd better stop looking to the heavens, waiting for help.

Many self-styled revolutionaries would tell you that we must adopt such an attitude if we're serious about changing the world. Yet in the years since I rejected white Jesus, I've had to recant the idea that the spiritual is essentially nonrevolutionary.

Assata Shakur complained about people like my former materialist self in her autobiography. She wrote about "pseudo-revolutionary robots" (ouch!) who attacked her comrade Lolita for her religious beliefs. "It apparently had never occurred to those fools that Lolita was more revolutionary than they could ever be, and that her religion had helped her to remain strong and committed all those years," she wrote. "I was infuriated by their crass, misguided arrogance."[10]

There isn't room in this book to detail how I got from weeping over God's death to having some sort of faith again. But I came to respect spirituality, even religion, again by reading the works of revolutionaries from around the world and by studying the history and practice of nonviolent struggle. I'll talk more about my self-directed study of revolutions later. For now, suffice to say that as I embarked on the journey to understand how ordinary people can work together to change the world, I kept running into spirituality, religion, and sometimes even Jesus.

I learned about the crucial role Muslim religious leaders and holidays played in the Iranian Revolution that deposed dictator Reza Pahlavi, the Shah;* about how the principle of *ahimsa* (do no harm) influenced Gandhi's nonviolent philosophy; and about how the writings of J.R.R. Tolkien were a source of inspiration for the leader of the nonviolent revolution that ousted Serbian dictator Slobodan Milošević. I read about Quakers who trekked miles on foot to campaign against slavery in the Americas and Christian pastors who walked the Trail of Tears with indigenous people. On a trip to the National Museum of African American History and Culture in Washington, D.C., I was moved as I

---

* It's important to note another authoritarian regime emerged from the nonviolent movement that deposed Reza Pahlavi. That's a highly unusual case, and it raises important questions about how movements fighting for justice are organized internally so they don't become the very thing they're fighting against. The most salient point here, though, is the role spirituality played in the movement's success.

stood in front of Nat Turner's Bible and Harriet Tubman's hymnal.

And if all that wasn't enough, my materialist position took another big hit when legal scholar and acclaimed author Michelle Alexander, who changed the way an entire generation understands the U.S. prison system with her book *The New Jim Crow*, joined the faculty at Union Theological Seminary as a visiting professor in 2016. She explained her decision by saying, "Without a moral or spiritual awakening, we will forever remain trapped in political games fueled by fear, greed and the hunger for power."[11]

Seeing all these ways spirituality fueled revolutionaries was a large part of what made me reconsider throwing spirituality away. I'm still recovering from the trauma of learning that the religion of my youth was founded upon anti-Blackness—that the people I used to worship alongside were basically singing to an imaginary white nationalist in the sky. I don't suspect I'll ever see the devout young Andre I used to be again. But I no longer subscribe to the popular notion that spirituality has no place in the revolution.

In his book *The End of Protest*, Occupy Wall Street co-founder Micah White puts it frankly: "In our global struggle to liberate humanity, the most significant battles will be fought on the spiritual level—inside our heads, within our imagination and deep in our collective unconscious."[12] So, if spirituality is important to you, you don't have to throw it away.

What is at stake in all of these conversations is the hope of divine aid. Does God—will God—intervene or help? I know that question isn't important to everyone. But the question remains salient because so many people still believe in God, and their beliefs about what God is doing, or will do, in response to racism informs political actions (or lack thereof).

When a man named Anthony McClain was shot in the back by the Pasadena Police Department as he fled from them in the fall of 2020, I spoke with some community members about what it might look like to come together and change policing in Pasadena. As soon as I began talking about the resources we'd need to gather to plan our first campaign, a Black woman cut me off to say, "I know God will take care of it."

I couldn't speak with the same confidence about what God would or wouldn't do. But I knew an effective campaign to disrupt police brutality in Pasadena wouldn't fall from the heavens. We would have to make those plans ourselves. I felt compassion for her, and I could sense that maybe I was overwhelming her with information. (My sister Myra tells me I can be like that: overwhelming.) I nodded at her response, knowing she didn't need a lecture on social movement theory from me, and we changed the subject.

I tell that story to spotlight how common and natural it is for many Black people to think theologically about our oppression. The notion that God is involved in our struggle and plays a role in it is common sense for many of us.

Since theology is an important factor in how many Black people frame and respond to our oppression, it's necessary to think theologically about how to invite Black people into the work to free ourselves. What we believe about divine intervention can make the difference between someone joining the movement, opposing it, or remaining inactive.

Some will take my spiritual journey as further evidence that white Jesus is standing in the way of Black liberation. In that sense, I would agree. White Jesus is a racist mythical character used to justify anti-Black violence. Black people who worship him tend not to fight for their freedom. But I disagree with those who conflate white Jesus with the divine in general.

There are ways that belief in divine intervention and political action can be compatible. I'm going to unpack an example using the Christian tradition, since that's the tradition most familiar to me. (May as well put these theology degrees to work!)

In the Hebrew Bible, God delegates authority to human beings to govern what happens on the Earth. "Rule over the fish in the sea and the birds in the sky and over every living creature that moves on the ground," God says to the first humans, according to the Book of Genesis. Later, the psalmist writes, "What is man that you are mindful of him? . . . You make him to rule over the works of Your hands; You have put all things under his feet."

This means that humans are called to participate directly in making history. We know that these scriptures imply political responsibility because, later in those same scriptures, the Hebrew prophets convey God's divine frustration at the social injustices in ancient Israel. God's frustration is rooted in the notion that humans have been deputized to rule the world and are accountable for what they do. "How long will you judge unjustly by granting favor to the wicked?" God asks them in Psalm 82. "Give justice to the lowly and the orphan; maintain the right of the poor and the destitute!" Note how the psalmist doesn't say, "God is on the throne, so don't you worry your pretty little head about politics." The message is, "God gave you this world; make it heaven."

It's an empowering message. When someone takes the command "Give justice to the lowly" to heart, they can confidently assume that God is working with them to do so. Many Black freedom fighters fought against white supremacy in that way, with the belief that God was the wind at their back. In this way, freedom movements can be seen as a form of divine intervention themselves, especially if we take seriously the idea that humans are bearers of the divine image.

In mapping out this theological argument, I don't mean to present a new dogma that all would-be revolutionaries must accept. I'm doing it to answer the question I asked myself for years after I left the church: *Do I need to throw spirituality away?* My answer is no. There are also many other spiritual and religious traditions that connect the divine and Black liberation: the Nation of Islam, Black Christian liberationist traditions, and Rastafari are a few that come to mind. Trying to take spirituality away from people for whom it is important is likely to just upset them. It's more realistic and useful to replace religious and theological frameworks that justify the status quo with ones that connect spirituality to social justice and prioritize the political liberation of the oppressed.

If spirituality isn't your bag, there's room for you too. The big lesson here for me has been for people to just respect each other's beliefs. The point of the revolution isn't to create an enclave where everyone shares all the exact same views but to work together for our freedom.

8

Revolution Now

"So you want to do something about racism," he smirked. "Which part?"

We'll call him Deon. He worked on Capitol Hill but was visiting Los Angeles for just a few days, and a mutual friend urged us to meet as soon as possible. So I lugged my boulder into a local coffee shop to meet him. If there were a dictionary entry for "Powerful Black Man," Deon's picture would've been next to it. He had ambassador swag: short and thin, clean-cut and sharply dressed in a crisp white shirt and suit jacket. And though he spoke softly and carefully, he exuded authority.

I think he could tell I didn't know how to respond to his question. So he pressed further.

"Well, do you want to do something about police brutality? Mass incarceration? Poverty? You need to pick something. Racism is too big and layered for the notion of 'fighting racism' to be meaningful. You need to choose an aspect of the system and commit all the facts to memory."

I took his advice seriously, but I had no idea how much it would change me. By the end of that summer, the apocalypse showed me that America's problems can't be solved by a few reforms here and there. If America wants to become a place where Black lives matter, everything about America will have to change.

Deon's guidance fell in line with my commitment to educate myself on systemic racism. Shortly after Philando Castile's death in the summer, I'd started a reading group with my friend Randell. Well, the reading group was more of an accident. I had found a reading list on racial justice and posted it on Facebook with the caption, "Who wants to get smarter?" People thought I was suggesting we read through some of the books together, and I went along with it.

We read broadly: everything from James Baldwin's *The Fire Next Time* to contemporary books like Bryan Stevenson's *Just Mercy*. It was like a survey class on racial justice for me. Through the many titles we read, I encountered mountains of research showing how racism affects economics, housing, infrastructure, healthcare—just about everything, really. I devoured information from other sources as well: articles, conversations with activists, TED Talks, academic lectures online, you name it.

I pondered Deon's questions for weeks. He'd made an excellent point. "Ending racism" is a noble goal, but it's not realistic until it's broken down into manageable bites. After a few months, I decided to focus on the criminal justice system, since that had been what provoked me to take action in the first place.

I pored over the work of legal experts and scholars, heeding

Deon's advice: commit the facts to memory. To do this, I built routines to educate myself. For example, I replaced my former habit of daily Bible reading with repeat viewings of Ava DuVernay's documentary *13th* on Netflix. I took notes, rewound sections to make sure I understood, and rehearsed the information: America holds 5 percent of the world's population but 25 percent of the world's prisoners, who are disproportionately Black. Black men account for 6.5 percent of the U.S. population but about 40 percent of the prison population. One in three Black men is expected to go to jail in his lifetime, in comparison to one in seventeen white males. I held these facts in mind like arrows in a quiver. Like I alluded to in the first chapter, the facts about America's racist history were a lot to take in. Every time I thought I couldn't be any more disappointed with America, some new fact about my country's racial cruelty would walk up and punch me in the chest. I wept a lot. Some days, I'd lose my appetite or just feel irritable.

Up to that point in my life, I think I expected to find racism in American society like one might find a paper jam. You open the printer and look for the lodged paper, so you can remove it and keep printing. Most Americans seem to view it that way—an otherwise healthy system experiencing temporary malfunctions. They see slavery, Jim Crow, and now the occasionally viral police killing as potholes in the otherwise smooth highway of racial progress. But the more I read about systemic racism, the more I learned about parts of American history that are widely unknown and seldom talked about. And I realized I had no idea of the depth of the *Maafa*'s violence.

There were all these gaps in the story for me. The two biggest ones were about the years between the end of chattel slavery and the Civil Rights Movement, and the years between the assassination of Dr. King and the present. I mean, I'd heard of landmark legislation like *Plessy v. Ferguson* but how Jim Crow segregation came to be? Couldn't tell you. And how did we go from King's murder to these viral police killings? Didn't know. In my reading, I found obscured histories that bridged the gaps.

I learned about the Black Codes, Jim Crow's predecessors, that took the baton from chattel slavery. Black Codes were created in Southern states to ensure newly liberated Black people would remain a source of cheap labor, just as they'd been during slavery, and the laws accomplished this by limiting their rights. In several states, Black Codes required African Americans to have written proof of employment on them at all times or else risk arrest or imprisonment, after which they could be leased to landowners as part of their sentence—a prerogative afforded to them by a loophole in the very amendment we're taught "abolished" slavery. This bit of history helped fill in the murky period between Emancipation and Jim Crow for me.

I read about the dismantling of Black political power during the Reconstruction era, the bombing of Black Wall Street in Tulsa, and the assistance police gave lynch mobs during Jim Crow. I read about how the FBI demolished the Black Panthers' Free Breakfast for Children program in the late 1960s, how the War on Drugs intentionally targeted Black people, and how police departments became more militarized in response to Black protests for racial justice. And that was just some of the information I absorbed in that time. Suffice to say that all of that history made clear how endemic racism is to American society.

In sum: I learned that for every victory won for racial progress in the U.S., there had been some counterstrike from white supremacy. And what was left of my belief in the dominant American narrative—the one that defined the American Way as truth and justice winning over oppression—gave way to a very different picture: one where racial injustice and inequality had always been the rails on which America's "democratic experiment" traveled. The experts exposed the idea that racism goes dormant like a virus and comes back seasonally as a misconception. Racism, they showed, adapts.

This apocalyptic process showed me that white supremacy, not democracy, is the American way that seeks to triumph and persevere against all odds. It has refused to be thwarted by the antislavery movement, the Civil Rights Movement, and now the Black Lives Matter movement. And if racism is a feature—not a bug—of the system we've inherited, then the system doesn't need some tinkering to work better. The system of oppression must be replaced with a system that can liberate. It needs radical change, fundamental change—a revolution.

Donald Trump's 2016 presidential win would cement my new understanding of America. If I had any doubts about the historical dance of racial progress and racist backlash, they were dispelled in 2016, when we all lived through the latter in real-time. "This is one of the most exciting nights of my life," former Grand Wizard of the Ku Klux Klan David Duke posted to Twitter the morning after Trump claimed the U.S. presidency. "Make no mistake about it, our people have played a HUGE role in electing Trump!"[1] In a *Vice News* documentary, genteel white nationalist Jared Taylor would later explain to author Eddie Huang:

I voted for Donald Trump for one reason only. His policies, if implemented, would slow the dispossession of whites in the United States. If you'd deport all illegal immigrants. If you were to think very hard about letting in any Muslims. All of this would slow the rate at which whites are becoming a minority. . . . We don't control China. . . . We don't control any place where whites are not a majority. If we become a minority, we won't control our own destiny anymore. When my ancestors built this nation they didn't build it with the intention of giving it away to Mexicans or Chinese or anything else.[2]

Donald Trump won the presidency because many white Americans shared the fears Taylor expressed. A 2016 poll from *The Washington Post* reported that Trump "did particularly well among people who said they are struggling economically, with 40 percent of their support, and even better—43 percent—among people who said that whites are losing out [because of the gains of other racial groups]."[3] Philip Klinkner, after analyzing the 2016 American National Election Study pilot survey, saw a similar trend: "Those who express more resentment toward African Americans, those who think the word 'violent' describes Muslims well, and those who believe President Obama is a Muslim have much more positive views of Trump."[4] *Atlantic* journalist Emma Green summarized post-election survey data collected by the Public Religion Research Institute, writing, "Besides partisan affiliation, it was cultural anxiety—feeling like a stranger in America, supporting the deportation of immigrants, and hesitating about educational investment—that best predicted support for Trump."[5] The numbers don't lie. White America voted for

Donald Trump to keep America a place where white lives matter most.

It's nice to have stats and studies on white support for Trump, but many Black people didn't need polling and reporting to know that a tidal wave of white racial anxiety carried the 45th president from Trump Tower to the Oval Office. We'd seen them cheer when their candidate promised to persecute Latino migrants, ban Muslims, and bully Black protesters. And these weren't even dog whistles anymore! The message was clear: he would save America from the threat of racial progress. "Watching the map turn red was like seeing one big 'Whites Only' sign appear," my friend Victor said. We were reminded once again that America's founders hadn't declared their beautiful democratic ideals with us in mind.

I wanted to believe in the idea of America that night. I fought to believe it. *There's no way he wins this election,* I kept saying to myself. Shaking my head. Smoothing my hair. Pacing the floor. *America is smarter than that,* I told myself. *There's no way we elect an overt racist to the highest office in the country—this is 2016, for crying out loud!* But America proved me wrong.

Whatever illusions I had that the values expressed in our Declaration of Independence reflected the true character of America, died that night. White America made it clear that they were more committed to whiteness than democracy.

"I am devastated," I posted on Facebook the next morning.

"Well, the other option was a criminal," retorted a friend I'll call Cash Humphrey.

Cash was part of another white family I'd adopted years before. I worked for his father, Garth, when I was in college and came to see him as a father figure—which made Cash my brother by extension. There was a time when I used to call Garth Humphrey on every holiday. If I lost track of time on Thanksgiving or Christmas and ended up calling Garth late in the evening, he'd often answer by saying, "I knew you'd call," with a smile in his voice. Eventually, I started calling Garth on the random holidays like Presidents' Day or Groundhog Day, just to have a good laugh.

But much like the Stones, the Humphreys and I had been drifting apart that summer as I embraced the antiracist movement. I'd spent hours on the phone with Garth, trying to reason with him about the many protests we'd seen in the news. But Garth didn't believe racism was a problem Black people were facing in America today. It pained me to see how a man I called "father" would struggle to believe or empathize with me.

Out of respect for Garth, I held back on Cash at first. "My lament is not an invitation to a debate," I told him. "This is your only warning." I hoped he'd go away at that.

He didn't.

"Not debating just stating facts lol. But thank you for the warning."

"Did you see the word 'devastated' in the original post?" I wrote. "Does it look like I am ready to LOL with you? Strike two."

Cash wrote back immediately, saying he "didn't understand" why I said I was devastated. His response was full of snark. For some reason, he also added that my education had no bearing on the conversation—just threw that in there to take me down a peg. He insisted that if I dare to state my "opinion" in public, I should brace myself for backlash.

I decided to call him.

I was enraged—sick and tired of men who've never lived a day in Black skin, never read a book about the Black struggle for freedom, never lifted a finger to fight against systemic racism, hurling their ignorance at me while I'm clearly in public grief. His audacity to read a statement about my emotional state back to me as an "opinion" he could debate set me off. I was done explaining my grief to people who simply didn't give a damn, people who wouldn't just use their reasoning skills to discern why a Black man would be disappointed that the president-elect was the KKK's dream candidate.

I'd tried signaling to Cash that I was expressing how I felt and not really looking for a political debate—twice! And he brushed my grief aside to fulfill some sick desire to dig his finger in the wound. It felt familiar, like that moment when Hunter sat back and smirked after telling me God won't help Black people get free.

My exchange with Cash was the final sign I needed to see that people who cling to whiteness can't love Black people. Their love would always evaporate when Black people lamented about anti-Black violence. I'd experienced it with my best friend in seminary when he argued on behalf of slavery. I'd heard it in the voice of Cash's father in those hours we spent arguing about the movement for Black lives, when I exhausted every persuasive strategy I could think of to convince him that racism was a matter of life or death for me—after which he'd tell me it wasn't real. I flashed back and saw that kitchen at Thanksgiving two years before, with most of the Stone children standing in silence after Guthrie told me to learn the white man's history.

Countless times, the white people I once called friends and family would go blank when they came face to face with Black pain. It was like one of those horror movies where the soul gets snatched out of someone. Like robots programmed to shut down whenever they hear the word *race*, they always went cold at the exact moment when I—their alleged "Black friend"—would have appreciated their empathy.

My relationship with the Stones broke for good around that time as well. We'd been distant since I had left them in Atlanta, but some of them had reached out to me by election time. Ashlee got in touch because she'd started working with a white-led anti–human trafficking organization that factored in race as part of its analysis of the issue. "I see both sides now," she exclaimed to me. Sally, Connor's wife, reached out to me after seeing *The Free State of Jones* starring Matthew McConaughey, a Civil War period film about a white abolitionist who led an armed revolt against the Confederacy. "When I first saw you with your boulder, I thought 'why is he stirring up trouble,'" she wrote to me, and then went on to tell me how McConaughey's performance convinced her that racism was a problem.

I sighed at their epiphanies. The white activists and actors they now praised hadn't told Sally and Ashlee anything they hadn't already heard from me. Yet their family, for some reason, dismissed what I'd said to Guthrie at Thanksgiving two years before, reprimanded me when I posted poems to Facebook during the Baltimore riots, and ignored me when I bared my pain the next year with the boulder and the suit jacket and the songs.

It was clear: they were always going to find the truth hard to believe if it didn't come from a white person. I realized that trying to get through to them would have little effect on them but would be a consistent source of frustration and disappointment for me. If it took three years just to get from "I thought you were stirring up trouble" to "racism exists," how could I know that they'd ever get to "America is fundamentally racist and needs radical change" within my lifetime? On the same day in November, I blocked all of the Humphreys and Stones.

As I write this now, it feels woefully inadequate to say that racial progress in America is always "one step forward, two steps back" as I was beginning to conclude back then. It's bigger than that—and deeper. America is an empire founded on racial violence and oppressive politics, an unequal society by design. It experiences prodemocracy uprisings from time to time that are violently put down by fascist counterrevolutions—and we are living through the latter today. Americans must reckon with the fact that America has been the world's leading producer of racist ideas and white supremacist violence for centuries.

America has been so proficient in its antidemocratic practices that, for much of its history, it has been a beacon for enemies of democracy around the world. In his 1934 *Völkische Weltgeschichte* (Ethnic History of the World), Nazi author Albrecht Wirth wrote, "The most important event in the history of the states of the Second Millennium . . . was the founding of the United States of America. The struggle of the Aryans for world domination thereby received its strongest prop."[6] You read that correctly. Third Reich Nazis saw something familiar and inspiring in America's politics and society. They identified the Ku Klux Klan as American fascists while praising the U.S. more generally for its discriminatory policies against Chinese immigrants, its Jim Crow laws, and its imperialist policies in the Philippines and Puerto Rico.

Just as Nazis found America's white supremacy familiar, Black Americans saw something familiar as they watched fascism sweep over Europe in the 1930s. Langston Hughes addressed the Second International Writers Conference in 1937, saying:

> We are the people who have long known in actual practice the meaning of the word fascism. . . . In many states of our country Negroes are not permitted to vote or hold office. . . . Freedom of movement is greatly hindered, especially if we happen to be sharecroppers. . . . We know what it is to be refused admittance to schools and colleges, to theatres and concert halls, to hotels and restaurants. . . . In America, Negroes do not have to be told what fascism is in action. We know.[7]

Dr. Martin Luther King Jr. made a similar observation in his 1967 book *Where Do We Go From Here: Chaos or Community?* that "America had a master race in the ante bellum South"; and many white Americans wanted to undo the gains of the Civil Rights Movement to establish "a native form of fascism."[8] Black Panther Party Leader Kathleen Cleaver wrote in her 1968 essay "Racism, Fascism, and Political Murder," "The advent of fascism in the United States is most clearly visible in the suppression of the black liberation struggle."[9] And that's without mentioning the many Black thinkers before 1930 who pointed out the chasm between America's democratic rhetoric and antidemocratic practice, or those who have continued to do so since the decline of the Civil Rights Movement in the 1970s.

"Whitelash," as political commentator Van Jones tearfully called it on CNN the morning after Trump won the presidency in 2016, is too soft a term. Many white people today are succumbing to a preventive fascism in response to the gains of the movement for Black lives, as they often have.

Some people say *fascist* is too extreme a label—that the term is overused and should only be applied to dictators, secret police, and concentration camps. But the editors of *The U.S. Antifascism Reader* are among the experts who define fascism as a militaristic "largely middle-class movement" that evokes a mythical past to call for national renewal, often through some mix of anti-Marxist, racist, and authoritarian rhetoric. "In addition, it actively mobilizes the population in a culture war against national minorities and/or the political left," they add.[10] Professor Louie Dean Valencia-García explains, "A more simplified definition of fascism, would be a sort of formula like: racism + anti-intellectualism + anti-liberalism/anti-socialism + xenophobia + ethnocentrism + nationalism + queerphobia + misogyny = fascism."[11] And we've been watching this equation come together throughout history.

When Black people gain more freedoms, the backlash begins. Accusations of Marxism and Communism proliferate, "law and order" rhetoric rises, armed white supremacist groups rise or reemerge, and white voters seem willing to put anyone in public office who will defend racial hierarchy. It's important to spell this out today, because we're witnessing it happen again in real time—from the tiki torch wielders in Charlottesville chanting the Nazi slogan "Blood and Soil" to the violent mob that attacked the U.S. Capitol in the Trump administration's final days chanting "U! S! A!"

There's no justifiable basis to look at the native fascism rising in America today and clutch our pearls, saying, "We're better than this," or "This isn't who we are." We're not better than this. It's always been "who we are." When we look at the attacks on Black life throughout the history of the United States, it is obvious that native forms of fascism, imperialism, authoritarianism, and even totalitarianism are part of America's political tradition. If the United States has been exceptional at anything, it's oppressive politics. We can look these facts in the face and chart a new course forward, or we can plug our ears and sing "The Star-Spangled Banner." But we do the latter to our own peril.

The fascist element in America's counterrevolutions threatens democracy for everyone, not just Black people. The off-duty cops who stormed the Capitol, for instance, demonstrated that an institution built to limit democracy for some can threaten democracy for all, as off-duty policemen brought the tools they usually use to put down Black Lives Matter protests—flex cuffs, batons, shields, pepper spray, and tear gas—to terrorize Congress. America tolerated white supremacy for generations, especially in law enforcement, and in 2021, white supremacy compelled law enforcement officers to attack American democracy at large. Once a weapon is built, there's no way of ensuring it will only be used on the enemies for whom it was first intended.

As I spent more time studying Black freedom struggles, I saw that I was undergoing a pattern that many Black activists share. Nearly all of the thinkers I admired had entered the racial justice struggle with a great deal of optimism about the possibilities for progress and about white people in general. But years of activist experience ended up tempering their optimism with some harsh truths. The most striking of these transformations for me was that of Dr. King.

Two interviews from the final years of Dr. King's life come to mind. The first one marks a change in his understanding of the scope of systemic racism and what kinds of measures were necessary to confront it. "For years I labored with the idea of reforming the existing institutions of the South, a little change here, a little change there," he told journalist David Halberstam in an April 1967 interview. "Now I feel quite differently. I think you've got to have a reconstruction of the entire society, a revolution of values."[12] In other words, King said he realized racism was a radical problem that required a radical solution.

Later that year, King told NBC News, "some of the old optimism was a little bit superficial. . . . Many of the people who supported us in Selma, in Birmingham, were really outraged about the extremist behavior toward Negroes, but they were not at that moment and they are not now committed to genuine equality for Negroes. . . . And this is where we're getting the resistance, because there was never any intention to go this far."[13] Dr. King had come to see how deeply entrenched white people were in their racism and came to the conclusion that "only a small minority" of white people were interested in genuine equality.

When I heard Dr. King utter the words above on YouTube, it resonated deeply with me. By calling out the scope of the problem and white people's lack of interest in solving it, King didn't mean there was no hope for change. (He made a point to tell interviewers that he remained hopeful.) However, it did signal to me that I should adopt a more realistic attitude toward the American system and white America. I had to accept that I'd been calling white Americans to be true to a specious democratic tradition that was always for whites only. I also had to accept that people like the Stones and the Humphreys will probably never actively fight racial inequality, because inequality is what makes whiteness meaningful.

If there is any American democratic tradition to hearken back to, it isn't found at the dinner tables of comfortable middle-class white people. It begins in the shacks of the enslaved and the sanctuaries of the disinherited, and is carried forward by Black abolitionists, intellectuals, artists, and activists who fought against imperial oppression. That tradition is primarily about organizing the oppressed and their allies for strong civil resistance. Just as King's objective for the final campaign of his life was to "cripple the operations of a repressive society" through nonviolent struggle, it became clear to me that contemporary racial justice activists must be determined to do the same.

The question I have today is whether or not all those millions of people who filled the streets in 2020 for George Floyd and Breonna Taylor have realized that their next task is to use nonviolent direct action to cripple the operations of a repressive society. We're not just fighting for white Americans to be nicer; we're fighting against a corrupt empire. We must connect the struggle for Black lives today to previous movements against imperialism, authoritarianism, and fascism around the world and at home. We must learn from those movements and apply their lessons to our situation today, with the understanding that tinkering with the current system isn't enough. The current system was built to oppress, which means it must be replaced. We must go from being a fundamentally unequal society sustained by violence to a truly egalitarian society sustained by mutual care. A revolution is necessary to make Black lives matter, and we have to plan it.

9

(White) Men Explain Things to Me

Candles of all heights and colors, flower bouquets, and pictures of J. R. Thomas lined the sidewalk where he was killed. I drove by that memorial on my commute to and from work every day, shaking my head each time I passed. Each time I saw his photo, I remembered what it felt like to hear the news he'd already been subdued when the police beat him to death.

I appreciated the memorial for Mr. Thomas but also felt it was unfair. The community would think of their beloved J.R. every time they saw the candles and pictures, but the police would have no such reminder. That gave me an idea: what if we could build a memorial to J. R. Thomas at the doors of the Pasadena police station, to display the grief of the community at the doorstep of those who had caused it? I spent a few weeks sharing the idea with a few friends, who all seemed excited about it. Then we started planning.

First, we needed to find the exact spot to place the memorial. I went with Mitch, a white friend, to scope out the police department's campus. On the way over, we talked about J.R.'s death, the movement, and about the possibility for change in Pasadena. Mitch paused, his voice lowered: "Are you ready to go to jail over this?"

"Yes," I said.

"Good. Me too."

We chuckled together.

We arrived at the police station and began to meander around, looking for an ideal spot for the memorial. "Look," Mitch called out, motioning at the ground. There was a police shield embedded in the floor with an inscription that read, HOW WE GET THE JOB DONE IS JUST AS IMPORTANT AS GETTING THE JOB DONE. We locked eyes. "Well, obviously it has to go here," Mitch said.

We figured the police would remove our display once it was built, so we devised a plan to make a memorial that would regenerate. When the city removed our photos and candles during the day, another memorial would take their place by evening. Mitch set up a Google Sheets where people could sign up for a slot, pick up a memorial-making kit, and assemble it at the police station.

At home, I created a graphic of J.R. and a brief summary of what had happened to him. Then I put out a call on social media for candles, plastic bags, incense sticks, matches, and other supplies to make memorial kits. Several people from all kinds of backgrounds responded—some I knew, others I didn't. They dropped off whatever supplies they had. Some stuck around to help me package the items in plastic baggies. Then we loaded them into a large Tupperware bin and set it on my front porch.

Since we planned to light candles and burn incense, we did some research on laws about vandalism and leaving an open flame at the police station. (We didn't want to break any laws without knowing, or without good reason.) We found it was illegal to leave an open flame unattended in public, so we asked participants to stay at the police station memorial until the incense burned out.

In case anyone is wondering, it takes a while for an incense stick to burn out—about forty-five minutes, to be exact. So if you're planning an action where an incense stick is your timer, plan accordingly. We found this out the awkward way, standing around the memorial in silence, not really sure how to fill the time, since we hadn't planned to spend an hour there. As we watched the candlelight flicker against J.R.'s picture, I could feel that we'd carried more than one death from one neighborhood with us. This was about the *Maafa*. I don't remember the silence being broken the first day we met there, as civilians periodically filed in and out of the police station doors. No officers passed through that entrance, and no personnel came out to address us. It was a surprisingly peaceful and cathartic hour.

After a few days of meeting, we naturally found ways to break the silence that felt appropriate and meaningful—songs, prayers, and just sharing whatever was on our hearts. That time of spontaneous sharing eventually developed into an organized weekly vigil at the police station doors.

Weeks passed, and as December approached, we decided to put the word out about the vigil more publicly, using the Christian holiday season of Advent as a frame. The forty days of Advent symbolize the centuries ancient Jews spent living in exile from their ancestral land, awaiting liberation from imperial oppression, which Christians believe culminated in the birth of Jesus. We felt Advent held space for anyone longing for liberation in the present day, so we invited clergy from several religious traditions to speak and musicians to lead songs at the memorial.

On the night of the first Advent vigil, I stood by the police station memorial while Mike Kinman, an Episcopal priest, smeared the ground with anointing oil. Mike had just moved to town from Ferguson, Missouri, where'd he been pulled into the Black Lives Matter movement in the wake of Mike Brown's death.

"So what are we calling this?" Mike asked.

"Well," I shrugged, "I've been calling it a subversive liturgy."

"I like that. All liturgies should be subversive," he replied with a smile.

My heart beat a little faster as I wondered if anyone would actually join us. But just as the hour to meet arrived, silhouettes began emerging from the shadows surrounding the station. About eighty people came from around the Los Angeles area that night to hold space for Black lives. It was the beginning of a month of gorgeous solidarity: people from all kinds of racial groups, religious traditions, and income brackets singing together, forming new friendships, and reflecting together on a revolution for racial justice.

By the end of the month, we felt so energized that we decided we'd continue the vigil for a year. We met regularly, raised some financial support for J. R. Thomas's family, and helped organize supplies to support the Black Lives Matter Pasadena Freedom School, which sought to offer public education for Black youth in the community. But one of the clearest examples of the power of that space was revealed to me in a conversation I had with my friend Becca, a white Pasadena resident, long after the vigils had stopped.

Some context: one Sunday afternoon, word went around that the lead organizer of Black Lives Matter Pasadena, Jasmine, had been arrested after someone falsely accused her of having a gun. We usually did our liturgy on Thursdays, but for Jasmine we called an emergency liturgy at the police station immediately. I don't know how many people showed up, but it was more than I'd ever seen at one of the gatherings. We wanted the police to know that whatever they did with Jasmine, the people of Pasadena would be paying attention. We also wanted Jasmine to know she wasn't alone. So we sang and chanted as loud as we could, inserting her name into old protest songs, stomping on the ground and clapping. When we decided to disperse, we let everyone know that Jasmine would be in court the next morning and that it was super important that everyone come to the courthouse to show up in support. Becca was there for all of this.

I wouldn't have pegged Becca as someone who'd show up for court support for a Black Lives Matter activist. She didn't come off as the activist type. She was a single mom of two, a wiz in nonprofit management, and an aspiring realtor who lived on the east side of town, where most people probably hadn't even heard about what happened to J. R. Thomas.

"Before coming to the liturgy," she told me, "the only things I knew about Jasmine came from the papers, and they didn't paint her in a flattering light." But Becca had gotten a glimpse of what Black residents in the redlined district of Northwest Pasadena really went through by hanging out at the subversive liturgy. She also got to see Jasmine a couple of times. Though the two never interacted directly, the gatherings gave Becca a chance to witness Jasmine's sincerity, courage, and deep love for her community up close.

"Before last year, did you ever imagine you'd be skipping work to make sure an activist wasn't unfairly charged?" I asked her.

"Absolutely not," she said. "I was really sheltered from the things people of color experience every day. The stories I heard at the liturgy were disturbing, but I knew I needed to keep showing up, to keep listening."

I swear, if it weren't for people like Mitch, Mike, Becca, and several others from the liturgy, I'd probably have written off white people altogether. But the liturgy brought me into community with new people who shared my values, even some white people. It turns out that this is often what happens: we may not be able to bring most of our loved ones through the apocalypse with us, but there's a post-apocalyptic community waiting for us on the other side.

At the same time, in the months that followed, the apocalypse had something to reveal to me about white liberals. By then, I'd stopped debating with the white conservatives I grew up around and focused my energy on things like running the liturgy, making educational videos, and writing new songs about Black life and racial justice. But the white people I'd learned to avoid were mostly external to the movement. I hadn't yet learned to watch out for the unkeepable white people who show up in movement spaces: namely, self-designated white "allies." The self-proclaimed white ally is often just as racist as the white opposers (though they'd hate to know it). We must learn to be aware of the ways these alleged allies show up, because otherwise they'll distract us from our revolutionary work with liberal white nonsense.

During the year we held the liturgy at the Pasadena police station, lots of new people were drawn into my orbit. Among the most eager of those newcomers were white men who just felt like they really understood racism. But too often, they'd presume to be advisers, offering to help me in unsolicited, sometimes patronizing, ways.

"I love you brother," a white PhD student at Fuller wrote to me. (White Christian men love prefacing their nonsense with brotherly love.) "You're right about racism being real, but I see some things posted recently and just feel the poison in them." We'll call him Dax. I knew of him at Fuller, but we'd never had a conversation before I graduated. Dax is one of those white guys who think they get it because they grew up around Black people and like R&B music. "I would like to talk about how to go about concretely helping black people in our country," he wrote.

Dax and I arranged a time to chat—the first of many conversations. It was clear after a few of them that Dax assumed I wanted to appeal to benevolent racists. I never got the opportunity to tell him that I'd cut off the benevolent racists I used to call family and wasn't interested in acquiring more. Then again, it never occurred to him to ask about my goals.

Dax had a habit of giving me information I already had. For example, I started to raise awareness about organizations working on solutions for police brutality. One morning, I posted the work of Campaign Zero, who'd put forward a platform to eliminate police killings. Their first policy suggestion was to end "broken windows policing," a crime management strategy that aims to prevent crime in general by targeting minor offenses. It's based on a criminological theory that says: "if a window in a building is broken and is left unrepaired, all the rest of the windows will soon be broken."[1] I was familiar with the broken windows theory and policing because I had read Malcolm Gladwell's book *The Tipping Point* in college, where he credits Mayor Rudy Giuliani's broken windows policies with dropping crime rates in New York City in the 1990s. Then I moved to New York a few years later and experienced the tactics Gladwell had written about firsthand.

"You know not everyone thinks broken windows policing is bad," Dax commented on my post. "You should read Malcolm Gladwell's *The Tipping Point*. He's got a lot in there about broken windows theory." I was a little puzzled that Dax assumed I wasn't familiar with a concept I was posting about. Not only was I familiar, but broken windows policing wasn't theoretical for me. It was something I experienced in my body, when police stopped and searched me.

I took Dax's whitesplaining with a grain of salt. I knew he meant well, so I just held space for him being a bit pedantic. But Dax wouldn't be able to hold space for my Black rage the way I did for him. Our friendship began to shift after a young woman named Korryn Gaines was killed by police in Maryland in the late summer of 2016.

Baltimore police had come to serve Ms. Gaines a warrant for an earlier traffic violation. When an officer kicked in the door, Gaines was sitting on the floor cradling her five-year-old son and a shotgun. She pointed the gun at the officer and told him to leave. That began a six-hour standoff with Baltimore SWAT, which culminated in them shooting at Gaines and her returning fire. She and her son were struck. She didn't survive.[2]

I posted Korryn Gaines's picture to Facebook with the caption, "I'm tired of hashtags." Dax was incensed. He was big mad that Black people were outraged at her death. "Did you guys read the article? You can't point a gun at cops and say you're going to kill them while holding a child on your lap. This is outrageous, but not because of what the cops did."

We hopped on the phone.

I tried to reason with him. What was most salient to me wasn't that Gaines had pointed a gun at the police. Plenty of white men have waved guns at officers and been taken into custody alive. There must have been more to the story.

If Dax had done a little digging, he'd have learned that Gaines wasn't just some reckless mother with a gun but an avid reader and self-taught student of political science from a law enforcement family. She'd been educating her neighbors about police brutality ever since Baltimore police murdered her neighbor Freddie Gray the year before. After a lifetime of watching corrupt power and violence in policing, she'd come to a radical analysis of state violence.[3] It was clear that because of all she'd experienced, witnessed, and studied, she felt hunted and was trying to protect herself and her family. On top of all that, Gaines was a person living with mental illness. I wouldn't have made the choices she did, but I could see how she got there.

Dax, like many white Americans, didn't care about her story. He wanted me to be outraged with him. Instead, I was curious—and my curiosity signaled that I wasn't the Black guy Dax had expected. I wasn't a centrist, feigning to be objective about current events, encouraging dispassionate, rational discussion between both sides. I'd chosen the side of persecuted Black people. I'd never try to justify anyone's actions on the basis of skin color alone, but I'd never jump to the worst conclusion about us, even if the worst conclusion was the nearest in reach.

Dax and I didn't part ways that day, but we stopped talking about race. By the end of 2016, we barely interacted anymore. I tried to keep in contact, but I was exhausted by a familiar dynamic.

Whenever one of my white friends was upset by the movement, I seemed to become the sole custodian of our relationship. Earlier that summer, when Kevin defended chattel slavery, I ended up reaching out to him to follow up. When Garth Humphrey dismissed white supremacy as a figment of my imagination and we parted ways, I wouldn't hear his voice again until I called him three years later. When white men got upset with something I'd said about racism, they would offer their numbers for me to call them, even though they were the ones who wanted the discussion—almost like they were calling me to the principal's office. Whenever they were put off by something about race, it fell on me to follow up and manage the relationship. Now, the same type of thing was happening with Dax.

In our conversations, I realized an inherent power dynamic at work: an internalized inferiority on my part and an internalized superiority on his part. I'm not saying it was his fault, but I wasn't ready to have an "ally" like him around, because I hadn't learned to tell white people that their discomfort is their responsibility. I was regressing with him, trying to manage his comfort and seeking his approval, as I did with white friends I'd already let go of. Even though he considered himself an active ally in the movement, he had to go.

"Hi," a guy we'll call Reagan randomly messaged me on Facebook.

"Hi there."

"It seems like you have focused your life in a similar direction as my own, though by different means," Reagan said.

Reagan began to tell me about his nonprofit incubator that provides nonprofit status to leaders as well as coaching for fund development. He acted like he wasn't trying to pitch his organization to me, but he kinda was.

I took the bait and arranged to meet with him at a steakhouse in the ritzy suburb of La Cañada. "We will meet in the center of the Lords of Empire," he said.

As we talked over lunch, it became clear that Reagan was one of those white people who think they get racism because they've spent time in a foreign country. He claimed to have experienced antiwhite race prejudice in Ethiopia. I can't remember the details of that discrimination today, but he choked up more than once while describing it to me. What I do remember is that Reagan used his experience to say Black people in America don't have it nearly as hard as he did in Ethiopia; therefore we should just be grateful and stop being so intense about our struggle here.

I wanted to clean my ears out. I hadn't expected that kind of meeting.

When he moved on to suggest that he groom me to be more palatable to his white, center-right, religious conservative donors, I screamed (under my breath). I don't even want to talk to that crowd, much less play Uncle Tom for them! Externally, I kept a calm demeanor and explained I was more interested in being clear about my efforts for change—no bait and switch. He was also diplomatic. He offered me some more information about his org, and we called it lunch.

From there, though, Reagan became one of those hyperactive white male commenters: the troll who thinks he's an ally. Every time I posted about racism—and I mean every time—he'd show up with unsolicited advice or some comment to undermine whatever I'd said.

One day he said something pretty insensitive under one of my posts. I can't remember what. All I remember is saying, "This is a teaching moment." He didn't like that. "Facebook is a public forum. It sounds like you want the public forum but for no one to comment something that would expand or oppose or critique," he wrote to me privately.

I asked for his number.

On the phone, Reagan complained that it was condescending of me to say that his racially insensitive comment provided a teaching moment. I tried to get Reagan to see the double-standard here. Ever since he reached out to me, in every conversation, he adopted the role of the superior party—the guide, the coach, the champion—never that of an equal. He always presumed to teach but was offended at the thought of being taught. He loved to critique whatever I said but hated to be critiqued by me. Why?

He couldn't answer. Instead, he just fell back into his story about how he was once mistreated by Black people in Ethiopia. His voice quavered. Tears flowed.

For the first time I can remember, I was unmoved by his pain. I'd seen this move before. Sherry, the first white person I'd ever cut off for being willfully obtuse, used to do that "I'm white and I've been to other countries therefore I know more about racism than Black Americans" thing, and many more tried it after her. Ashlee Stone had also tried a version of this approach, when she told me a Black man had assaulted her—"I've been hurt by Black people, so Black people should just pipe down." I wasn't going to be distracted by white tears again. I find it spectacular how consistent and predictable white nonsense can be, yet every white person who spews it does so as though they're the first to ever make that argument.

"I'm sorry you had a hard time in Ethiopia," I said to him. "But that doesn't erase the systemic violence Black people are facing in this country." And though I still believe that answer, I wish I'd been more honest than that. Because the truth is, it didn't matter what Reagan had gone through in Ethiopia. And the mere fact that I had said "I'm sorry you went through that" seemed to enable Reagan to forget that this conversation had come about because *he* had said something racist. He sniffled, said "I feel better now," and got off the phone. Then he resumed his regular trolling.

That January, I put the word out that I wanted to do a film series for Black History Month. I asked my Black friends to vote on Black movies every Black person has to see to before they die. Once the results were in, we could watch them in my back-yard throughout the month of February.

Reagan sent me a message: "I am noticing your invitation to movie night is only for black friends but posted on facebook for all your 'white' friends to see. What message are you trying to send? What do you expect to happen relationally?"

"Again, these aren't conversations for FB messenger," I replied.

"Sorry can't talk now. Just got back from funeral," he said.

I just need to break the flow of this story and name that white men seem to love to do this. They lob some critique into a race conversation and then claim they're too busy to follow up on it. When someone calls them out, they're always at a funeral, or driving, or their wife is telling them to get off the phone. I think the truth is they never expect to converse about their thoughts because they have an unearned sense of authority: "I have spoken."

I told Reagan, "Everything isn't always about how white people feel about it." Then I went about my business.

I tell these stories about Dax and Reagan to illustrate how exhausting white "allies" can be.

Research suggests that white racial justice activists contribute to burnout for Black activists and those of color. A 2019 study summarizes the feedback of several nonwhite racial justice activists, who named white would-be allies—not just white people in general—as a primary stressor in their work. They identified five major ways white antiracist activists make our work harder: "(1) harboring unevolved or racist views, (2) undermining or invalidating the racial justice work of activists of color, (3) being unwilling to step up and take action when needed, (4) exhibiting white fragility, and (5) taking credit for participants' racial justice work and ideas."[4]

The findings of those recent studies are consistent with what we've seen in racial justice efforts over time. After the 1964 Freedom Summer project, in which white Civil Rights sympathizers joined the Black activists of the Student Nonviolent Coordinating Committee (SNCC) in rural Mississippi to register Black voters, Black activists also identified the racism of white allies as a stressor and an obstacle to their work. Before Freedom Summer, SNCC had envisioned the aftermath of the Civil Rights Movement as a "Beloved Community," where Black and non-Black people would live in harmony. But by the end of that summer, racial tensions within the movement had led many Black Civil Rights activists to become disillusioned about the prospect of Beloved Community and adopt a more radical, separatist outlook. Black interviewees reported that their white allies arrived in Mississippi with a superiority complex, racial insensitivity, and sexism.* One Black Freedom Summer participant wrote in his journal about some of the white volunteers: "generally a good bunch, but there were . . . a few who just came in and wanted to take over. Their attitude was 'okay, we are here, your troubles are over. We are going to put your house in order.'"[5] White allies continue to show up in a similar way today, as overseers instead of comrades.

This problem crosses borders, just as it spans generations. Olivia Alaso and Kelsey Nielsen co-founded Kusimama Africa, a Ugandan-based social justice organization that advocates for healthcare and against human trafficking. Through their media platform, "No White Saviors," they aim to "disrupt the White Savior Complex in international development and amplify the voices of those who are transforming their own communities," according to their website.

In an interview on my podcast, Olivia recounted how white

---

* Issues of gender and sexuality in Black freedom movements of the twentieth century are complicated. There's tension between Black men and white women activists; conflict between Black male and female activists; frustrations between Black and white women activists; and more tension around Black LGBTQ leadership. These challenges highlight the importance of intersectional analyses of oppression.

organizations enter her home country and deem the Ugandan organizations corrupt and "not on standard."[6] They then set up their own white-led organizations, with all-white board members, and place token Black faces in middle management who are leaders in title but have no real institutional power.

In Olivia's experience, white outsiders assume Ugandans can't accomplish the work white people can. "People feel that Africa needs saving all the time, and that Africa is in bad shape, so we need people to come to Africa and save our children and take them overseas," she adds. "They're not thinking about you— about how you feel. They're not listening to you."

I could hear the deep frustration in Olivia's voice as she spoke to me. In her own words, she'd echoed what SNCC activists said about the white saviors who'd come from the North to help them fight the Jim Crow system: these white people have appointed themselves our "allies," but they still think they know better than us.

So here's my point: watch out for white liberals. They can be just as much an obstacle to racial progress as their conservative counterparts. They may know all the latest social justice lingo, but they'll often use it to undermine whatever Black people say. When you speak frankly from your anger about racism, they'll pat you on the shoulder and coach you about how they agree with your sentiment but your tone is counterproductive. Many of them know how to make a concerned face as you vent, but they often won't take any steps that will actually disrupt existing racial power dynamics or inequalities. There are a lot of white people who are genuinely aggrieved at the gruesome spectacles of police violence that have become so common in recent years, but they aren't interested in radical change.

Another thing to watch out for: white people often use whatever proximity they have to Black folks as evidence that they've arrived at racial enlightenment and no longer need to examine themselves for anti-Black attitudes or behaviors. The very fact that they're involved in a racial justice activist group or antiracist book club can easily become their shield from any feedback on their problematic behavior.

I've had to deal with white allies who play devil's advocate to every plan Black activists formulate, white folks who constantly talk over people of color and eat up time at organizing meetings with long virtue-signaling rants, and even one white woman who asked one of our Black leaders if she could have permission to say "the N-word," I guess as a reward for all of her volunteer hours. I've also had to deal with white people who develop weird romantic obsessions with Black activists, to the point where it borders on stalking. I'm not saying these white people have nefarious motives, but they haven't addressed their superiority complexes, their deep suspicions of Black wisdom, or sexual fetishes, to name just a few examples.

And they're often just as fragile as their white conservative counterparts. When confronted about their harmful behavior, they'll often retort with some version of "Don't fight your allies, dude," as though we should just be grateful they bothered to show up. This may sound harsh, but Black activists should seriously consider asking problematic white allies to leave their groups if their behavior is consistently disruptive and harmful—especially if the person isn't open to feedback. They can always join a consciousness-raising group for white people seeking to unlearn anti-Blackness.

If white people are serious about fighting white supremacy and anti-Blackness, they need to start within themselves. This kind of work is essential because without it, white people will enter movement spaces and cause the same kinds of harm Black people are trying to get away from. They need to confront the ways they've been shaped by anti-Black ideas and been complicit in defending the racial hierarchy. They need to dedicate themselves to the work of fighting against racism in their own communities, instead of rushing straight into spaces where Black people are trying to heal and organize for our own freedom.

White people should consider how they can organize for racial justice in ways that give Black people space: space where we're free from the pressure to educate them, perform for them, or coddle them. One option is for white people to join non-Black ally movement groups that work in parallel with Black-led organizations and are accountable to trusted Black leaders: White People for Black Lives (WP4BL) or Showing Up for Racial Justice (SURJ), for instance. White people who really get it understand that such space is necessary.

Finally, white people should stop self-designating themselves as allies in the struggle for Black freedom. It's Black people's prerogative to name our allies when we recognize them, and not a moment sooner. We determine what's helpful to us. People who are serious about working alongside us will consider our feedback about how their presence is being received and adjust their approach where appropriate. Folks who act as though any feedback is a sign of ingratitude can stay home.

We don't need saviors. We need people who understand the subtle ways white supremacy and anti-Blackness control white people's behavior and who want to be free of their influence. As artist and activist Lilla Watson once said, "If you have come here to help me you are wasting your time, but if you have come because your liberation is bound up with mine, then let us work together."

10

How to Be Hopeful

It happened again.

In Dallas this time.

Fifteen-year-old Jordan Edwards was leaving a house party with four friends because they felt it was getting a little rowdy. That's when police arrived. Officers later said they were responding to a 911 call about "drunk teenagers" and a report of shots fired. But witnesses contradicted that report. They say no bullets flew that day until the police fired the multiple rounds that killed Jordan Edwards.[1]

The wake of Mr. Edwards's killing was the heaviest time I remember at our year-long Pasadena vigil. So much in the news cycle seemed to signal that America's anti-Blackness was getting worse: we had a president whose racist rhetoric seemed to grow more flagrant by the day, and the names of Black people slain by law enforcement kept rolling in. We were exhausted.

In addition to headline fatigue, I was also carrying the recent loss of my mother to pancreatic cancer. She'd been sick for years, but I only learned of the severity of her condition a few months before she passed.

In my college years, I'd made it a point to get to know Mackie better as a person. We would sit on the phone, and I'd ask her all about her life as a young girl in Kingston, where Mumma sent her to board with another family.* What did she like to do? Who were her favorite bands? It turned out that my mom loved to sneak into dance clubs and dance to the Beatles when she was young. So I made it a point to dance with her whenever I passed through Atlanta.

The last time we danced was at my sister's wedding two years earlier. Ever since, I'd kept hope alive that I'd get to turn on "I Want to Hold Your Hand" and do the Monkey with her one last time. But I never made the time or found the money to make that trip to Atlanta before she passed, and it was hard to forgive myself for it.

Like my grandmother, Mackie didn't want to be buried in the U.S. She wanted to rest next to her uncle and mother on a little plot of land my family owns in the rural parish of St. Elizabeth, Jamaica. So we respected her wishes, just as we had respected Mumma's, and held funerals both in Atlanta and in Jamaica.

Being back in Jamaica felt bittersweet. Growing up, my mother brought me and my siblings to the island on a regular basis so we'd know our heritage and our extended family. We went back every other year until the big recession in 2008 made it unaffordable. As a boy, I felt proud to be Jamaican but didn't

---

* I know this can be confusing. In Jamaica, it was normal for kids to be sent to board with other families. My grandmother is from a rural part of Jamaica called St. Elizabeth, but she sent Mackie, my mom, to board with a family in Kingston as a young girl.

appreciate our trips to the actual country so much. We never visited the Jamaica Americans fantasize about—the all-inclusive beach resorts, parasailing excursions, and all that. My family's Jamaica meant trekking barefoot up a dirt path to bathe in a nearby river in Spanish Town, or sleeping under a net attached to a ceiling fan to ward off Kingston's gangster mosquitos, or our whole family sharing one pot of pumpkin soup on Treasure Beach. Those family trips showed me that Jamaican life could be very difficult. It also didn't seem like a place I was welcome. Memories of my Jamaican cousins calling me *yankie* and *fahrinnah* (foreigner) come to mind. But the trip to lay my mother to rest with my ancestors was different.

My family on the island turned out to be a balm to my grief-stricken heart. There was something healing about sitting in silence with my cousins under the ackee tree in their front yard, watching hummingbirds dart through the bushes with a Red Stripe Lemon Paradise in my hand as a cool breeze gently massaged my skin—almost like we were sitting shiva, Jamaican style. My dreadlocked cousin Dale taught me some basic rasta dancing moves under the stars one night—and out in the country, you could see every single one of them. "Jamaica way!" he howled at the moon. I howled with him. And for the first time, Jamaica felt like home.

That week, we buried my mother in a spot surrounded by red clay, as red as the clay in Georgia where I grew up. Visiting it, I wondered if Georgia's red soil reminded Mackie of there, and if that's partly why she chose to raise us in Stone Mountain. The clay was so rich it stained my shoes, and I was glad for it. I'd be leaving my mom in Jamaica, but it felt like I was bringing a piece of her back with me.

After her funeral, my family loaded up the car and drove back to Montego Bay, where we stayed two more nights. We went to Doctor's Cave Beach the next day—on the "hip strip" where lots of tourists hang out—and sat on the beach eating jerk chicken and festival (a kind of long Jamaican fried dumpling with cinnamon) while sapphire waters tickled the shore just a few feet away. "Couldn't I just find a job here entertaining tourists?" I chuckled to my sister Myra. I was only halfway joking. I didn't want to leave. Jamaica felt spacious in a way I hadn't remembered feeling since the apocalypse began.

But when I came home, the feeling didn't last.

I spent a lot of time on my living room floor in tears in those days. If it wasn't one thing, it was another: another headline about police killing, another hidden history of racial violence uncovered, and of course, grief over my mom.

I'd spent a lot of energy in public grief about racism that year—the boulder, the suit, the songs I wrote. And the constant outrage and grief were catching up with me, becoming unmanageable. My drive to keep going was waning and my friends could tell.

One day a package arrived at my door from my friend Paul, an English professor in Central Florida. It was a book by activist Rebecca Solnit called *Hope in the Dark*. The book had meant a lot to him, and since he'd been watching my journey for several years, he sensed I'd appreciate it too.

I was skeptical about a book on hope. It seemed inappropriate and impossible, as I continued to mourn so much. I thought hope was some feeling that tells you, no matter what, everything is going to work out fine. But I had no reason to believe that. It seemed America had flat-out ignored the Black Lives Matter movement and elected an outspoken racist to the presidency, all while the police's Black body count continued to grow. It seemed like the movement was failing.

Frankly, I thought hope was bullshit. Mostly because all of the hopeful people I knew had a tendency to minimize problems in order to stay positive. It seemed that the only people I knew who had hope weren't paying close attention to what's going on in the world. *Hope in the Dark* was the beginning of a journey that would permanently shift my perspective.

The idea that struck me most in Solnit's book was that there's a difference between hope and certainty. To be hopeful doesn't mean we're sure about the future. "Hope is an embrace of the unknown and the unknowable, an alternative to the certainty of both optimists and pessimists," she explains. "Optimists think it will all be fine without our involvement; pessimists adopt the opposite position; both excuse themselves from acting."[2] My mouth dropped open when I first read those words. They gave me a concept of hope that looked ugly truths in the face and left room for human agency. It felt like good news.

From then on, I began to search for hope with the same resolve that I'd searched for information about racism. I developed a routine of morning and weekend hope readings that did wonders for my mental health and convinced me that true, meaningful hope—the kind that is grounded in history, able to confront uncomfortable reality, and comfortable embracing ambiguity—can be cultivated. Writings on hope from freedom fighters, past and present, became my holy texts. I would read them every morning or sneak away on my lunch break to pore over their words at my favorite burger spot. Somewhere in the turmoil of those months, my perspective shifted from thinking hope is bullshit to seeing hope as the fuel of revolution—an important lesson for all freedom fighters.

Movements for social change are more likely to happen when people believe their efforts will be worthwhile. If people see their votes as useless or think the authorities will always squash uprisings, they're less likely to take action to create change. This is because people pick fights they believe they can win.

Sociologist Doug McAdam reports that social movements are often triggered by what he calls "cognitive liberation."[3] Cognitive liberation, he explains, is the process by which people come to see their situation as both unjust and changeable. The first part of that equation—revealing injustices—is something activists try to do through their protests and symbolic actions. The second part is often communicated to the public through signals that the status quo is shifting.

The Civil Rights uprisings of the 1950s and the 1960s may have been partly inspired by a set of executive orders that addressed segregation in the U.S. Armed Forces in the 1940s.[4] In 1941, A. Philip Randolph and other Black Civil Rights leaders planned a massive March on Washington to protest discrimination in the defense industry. The march was called off when President Franklin D. Roosevelt issued Executive Order 8802, proclaiming, "it is the duty of employers and of labor organizations . . . to provide for the full and equitable participation of all workers in defense industries, without discrimination because of race, creed, color, or national origin." Later, the Committee

Against Jim Crow in Military Service and Training pressured President Harry S. Truman to expand on Roosevelt's order with Executive Order 9981 (1948), which called for the complete end of segregation in the U.S. Armed Forces.

These orders signaled to many Black Americans that the Jim Crow establishment was vulnerable to collective action. By 1955, the year of the Montgomery Bus Boycott, Civil Rights activists didn't have to wonder if change through collective action was possible. They'd seen it happen in recent memory.

Stories like this suggest that hope isn't just some mysterious, innate quality or emotion. Hope takes cues from current events and serves as the basis for action. Therefore, the kind of hope that is useful for social progress can't be found by people who bury their heads in the sand. It comes to people who are paying attention to what's going on in the world.

There's a snag here. The news media is notoriously negative. If we're watching major news outlets for cues that the status quo is vulnerable to collective action, we may never get them. Major news media outlets often report on social movements in the U.S. as though they're unnecessary, fruitless, or criminal—and they underreport on social movements happening around the globe.

This has meant that I've had to look for alternative media sources and curate the media I consume. I follow independent digital media sources that report on social movements and freedom struggles around the world, like the Center for Applied Nonviolent Action and Strategies (CANVAS) and *Waging Nonviolence.* Now I find that I'm the nerd at your dinner party who's weirdly attuned to the fact that democracies have been backsliding around the globe for years—but also energized by the creative protests happening in some country you may not have heard of. It may make me a little annoying, but looking for hope in this way—namely, by tracking freedom struggles—is a huge part of what keeps me going.

Knowledge of history is another essential ingredient in hope, because the past often illustrates what is possible for us in the present. Throughout history, freedom movements have inspired other freedom movements. In their struggle against apartheid, for example, the early African National Congress took inspiration from Gandhi's nonviolent movement against British rule. The U.S. Civil Rights Movement was inspired in part by decolonization struggles happening around the world at the time. The nonviolent movement that ousted Serbian dictator Slobodan Milošević looked back on the U.S. Civil Rights struggle for encouragement. When we remember the stories of people power overcoming oppression in the past, it serves as the grounds for hope that it can happen again.

For this reason, I define hope not as a feeling but as a conviction, based on the knowledge of all the ordinary people who have won against injustice before. The word *conviction* is based on the same root as the word *convince*. History and data have convinced me that change, from the bottom up, is possible. That is what hope means to me.

I emphasize the word *possible*. Hope is not the unqualified belief that victory is certain. That's presumption. True hope remains humble about the future, even as it continues believing in human agency. I'm hopeful because I believe history is a story we're writing together, not something happening to us—which means we all get a say in how the story ends. But that also means we're going to have to struggle for the story we want.

This conviction that we can win isn't static. It's a flame that must be fed and tended. We tend our hope by setting boundaries about how we consume news content that makes us feel despair. For instance, I made a decision in 2017 that I would no longer watch the video footage of a police killing—I know many others who did the same. Keeping that commitment has definitely made the way I pay attention to racial injustice more manageable.

There are many practical ways we can feed our hope. We surround ourselves with people who share our values, whose presence throws fuel on our fire. We honor our need to take breaks. We keep in mind that the completion of the struggle doesn't rest on the power of one individual—me or you—but on the collective. And most of all, we treat hope like a habit rather than a feeling. We develop a hope regimen, because hope is too important to revolution to let it happen by accident.

Here's what my hope regimen looks like. When I'm really disciplined, my laptop stays in another room while I sleep, and my cellphone doesn't rest next to my head during the night. I do this so that I'm not confronted with bad news first thing in the morning. When I wake up, I put on some music because it brings me joy, have a glass of water with lime, eat a small breakfast, and do a little cleaning. Then I sit down to read from whatever book about hope I have at the time (and I make sure I always have a book about hope). I've spent the past few years slowly reading a collection of essays edited by Paul Rogat Loeb called *The Impossible Will Take a Little While*, which I absolutely recommend to every person involved in some fight for a better world. When I'm done reading, I add lines that resonated with me to a list of "Hope Notes" I keep. I meditate for a few minutes, do a little exercise, then shower. Once I've dressed for the day, I'm now available to engage the news cycle and whatever is trending on social media—not a moment before.

Then there's my music. Though I've been making music since grade school, I've never been more grateful for music and the role it plays in my life than I am today. I remember the very moment this shifted for me, sitting alone at my piano, a few weeks after I started lugging the boulder around town, singing through a tightened throat:

It doesn't have to be this way!
It doesn't have to be this way!
It doesn't have to be this way!

I knew in that moment that I'd stumbled upon more than a catchy hook. I'd summarized everything I was learning about hope, nonviolent struggle, and systemic oppression in a single lyrical phrase. Since then, that refrain has become my life's motto. Songwriting has become an outlet for my feelings about living in this anti-Black world in this Black body. It's also become a balm for the stress of being aware of so much injustice, and sometimes even an escape from feeling heavy-hearted. Before the apocalypse, music was something I loved to do. On this side of the apocalypse, music is my lifeline. It's my greatest form of soul care.

You may have noticed that most of my hope regimen is just taking good care of my body, brain, and space. I can't explain why all of those things help manage hope for me. All I can say is that they've often kept me from despair. What works for you may be different. That's okay. The important thing is for you to find your hope regimen.

My early days as a racial justice advocate were fueled almost entirely by anger, outrage, and obligation. I thought I was supposed to be really serious and full of grief all the time, to match the seriousness of the problem we're fighting. But engaging the work through grief alone left me paralyzed with despair. The near–nervous breakdown I described before taught me that outrage, anger, and obligation won't sustain us in this fight.

Don't get me wrong: anger, outrage, and a sense of duty have their merits, but they also have serious liabilities. Outrage is a good sign that we're paying attention to what's going on in the world, but being outraged all the time robs us of time for joy and rest. Like I said in an earlier chapter, anger provokes us to act, but also drains a lot of energy. Obligation can motivate us to keep showing up to protests and other justice work, but it can cause us to hold poor boundaries that make us overextend ourselves in the name of the movement.

Here's another thing: outrage and anger can be unreliable motivators. They depend on some kind of tragic event to trigger an emotional reaction from the public. When the wave of anger recedes—and it will—a bunch of exhausted people retire from activism, many of them feeling that they marched their Achilles sore without much to show for it. The folks who keep organizing are left awaiting the next wave of outrage to inspire people to act. Part of what I've described is just a bad community organizing model, but I've watched that cycle be the norm in movement spaces for years now.

The best freedom fighters understand that people need something to believe in. Yelling "Where is your outrage?" doesn't work nearly as well as presenting a frustrated, persecuted people a compelling vision of what the world could be like if they'll organize themselves for sustained resistance. That was exactly how I started this journey. Yes, I was frustrated about my own experiences of racism and outraged by the news, but ultimately it was the knowledge that my predecessors forced the Jim Crow system to change that got me out into the streets. Anger pulled me toward this work, but hope has kept me in it for years.

For these reasons, I can't stress enough how important it is that the movement for Black freedom take hope seriously. We must become masters at cultivating it, because without hope, there will be no revolution.

PART III

Singing the Future

We are like gods and don't even know it,

Whatever we do becomes history,

They may have the guns but we've got the poets,

The future will be whatever we sing.

—"IT DOESN'T HAVE TO BE THIS WAY" (REMIX)

*Written in 2021 as I reflected on my part in the
George Floyd protests the previous summer*

11

The Truth About Unity

In the fall of 2017, I stuffed my silver Kia Rio with all my earthly belongings and began the five-day drive from SoCal to Central Florida. I'd been offered the position of managing editor at *Relevant,* a magazine and media group based in Orlando. Accepting the job had been a no-brainer, since I'd been a long-time fan of their content. In my interview, the CEO and the brand manager told me that they'd seen the social justice content I'd been creating online, and they were excited for me to bring that perspective to their platform, since justice was one of their areas of focus.

A few months into the job, I wrote an online story about Colin Kaepernick's kneeling protest against police brutality, which was still in the news. The Seattle Seahawks had reneged on giving Kaepernick a tryout because he wouldn't promise them he'd stand for the national anthem if they contracted him. He hadn't stood for the anthem since 2016 and had been blackballed from the league ever since. Even though an army vet had originally convinced Kaepernick to kneel instead of sit, feeling it would be more respectful to fallen soldiers, the quarterback's silent kneeling protest was still polarizing.

The angry comments I got on my news slice tracked with the controversy about Kaepernick's kneeling protest at large. A 2018 poll from NBC and *The Wall Street Journal* reported that 54 percent of Americans felt it was "inappropriate" for NFL players to kneel in silent protest of police brutality.[1] They also reported that 7 in 10 Black voters deemed Kaepernick's protest appropriate, in comparison to just 38 percent of white voters. It's amazing how Colin Kaepernick's silent protest became one of the most controversial actions of the Black Lives Matter era. Kaepernick received death threats from angry NFL fans. Angry customers posted videos online of them burning their Nike products when the athletics company inked a deal with Kaepernick later that year. His kneeling protest even provoked the ire of the president, who told Fox News, "You have to stand proudly for the national anthem or you shouldn't be playing, you shouldn't be there, maybe you shouldn't be in the country."[2] The vitriol Kaepernick received for kneeling in silence smacked of familiarity to many Black people who've been called "divisive" for speaking up about racism.

Much of white America seems to believe that racial justice depends on Black people becoming model minorities who save white America from its sickness of white supremacy by bringing people together for patient and loving dialogue. When we fail or refuse to conform to the model they've made for us, they call us divisive, yet another euphemism for "Bad Negro." They suggest that, if we're serious about racial progress, we'd better learn how to attract white people and keep them engaged.

If I had ten dollars for every time a white person accused me of being divisive, I'd be Jeff Bezos. White people have called me a racist, accused me of being "what's wrong with this country," and even randomly brought Dr. Martin Luther King Jr. into it to suggest he'd be ashamed of me. They say these things because they assume the fight for racial justice is about Black people, indigenous people, and people of color "coming to the table" and building bridges with them. But an apocalyptic journey through the work of iconic freedom fighters that year would prove that "coming to the table" is overrated.

I spent most of my time outside of my office with my nose in books written by freedom fighters. After work, I'd heat up some dinner in the microwave, watch an episode of *The Handmaid's Tale,* and then get to studying. I had compiled a reading list for myself on the topic of nonviolent struggle. At first, I just wanted to understand Dr. Martin Luther King Jr.'s intellectual influences. But that seed of curiosity would end up taking me on a journey from the antebellum period up to the present day.

I traced Dr. King's influences on direct action as far back as *Civil Disobedience,* in which Henry David Thoreau blasts the U.S. for chattel slavery and condemns the Mexican-American War as an indefensible example of American imperialist aggression. Thoreau led me to the works of Russian author and anti-war advocate Leo Tolstoy, who denounced policing and war, encouraging total noncooperation with evil. Tolstoy's work led me to Mohandas K. Gandhi's experiments with nonviolent resistance, first as a lawyer in apartheid South Africa, then against British imperialism in India. I followed Gandhi's influence to

Nelson Mandela's autobiography, learning how the African National Congress tried to follow Gandhi's example and why they ultimately abandoned it. From there, I pored over Dr. King's writings at night, often staying up until the wee hours of the morning.

While tracing this intellectual genealogy of nonviolence, I noticed some trends. One was the connection between racism, imperialism, and authoritarianism. This led me to the work of the iconic nonviolent strategist Gene Sharp, whose book *From Dictatorship to Democracy: A Conceptual Framework for Liberation* had been used to launch successful nonviolent struggles against totalitarian regimes around the world. Sharp's work introduced me to the story of the Rosenstrasse protest, where a crowd of unarmed ordinary women pressured Nazi soldiers to return their Jewish husbands to them—a story I cherish to this day.

I traced the trail to more recent uprisings: the color revolutions of Eastern Europe, the Arab Spring, the Occupy movement, Black Lives Matter, and many more prodemocracy movements around the world. It was a crash course in the history and practice of nonviolent struggle.

The greatest gift of my journey through these works was seeing how freedom fighters across time and space demonstrated that violent oppressors could be deposed by ordinary people who have nothing near the resources to match their oppressors' capacity for violence. Many Black people are given a whitewashed version of nonviolence that seems impotent and impractical, leaving us to conclude that only violence—a level of violence we don't have the resources to organize—could possibly liberate us. But nonviolent struggle can be a pragmatic, strategic choice when conventional warfare is just not a realistic option, whether for lack of allies, weapons, trained combatants, money, or any of the other resources that win wars. It's a different weapons system that allows all kinds of people in society to participate. It was a relief to me personally, because I would be a terrible soldier in an armed struggle.

Some of the most convincing data on nonviolent struggle comes from the research I mentioned in an earlier chapter from Maria J. Stephan and Erica Chenoweth that contained the 3.5 percent rule. Their study of 323 conflict situations between 1900 and 2006 also found:

- Nonviolent movements proved to be about twice as successful as armed struggles. According to the study, armed struggles have a 26 percent chance at success, while nonviolent campaigns have a 53 percent chance.[*]
- Revolutions achieved through arms showed a 5 percent chance of becoming democratic and a 43 percent chance of descending into civil war within ten years. Countries that experienced nonviolent resistance showed a 40 percent chance of becoming democratic and a 28 percent chance of civil war.[3]

But here's the thing: in all of my study and experience in nonviolent struggle, I can find no basis for white people's mis-

---

[*] In "The Demons of Violence" chapter of *Blueprint for Revolution* (244–267), Srdja Popovic adds, "If you look at the same statistics in the last two decades alone—with no more Cold War to spur the financing of armed conflicts across the globe—the ratio spikes even more dramatically in favor of nonviolence."

conception that social change is brought about through civil conversations and "peaceful" protests.

Everything I've read on nonviolent struggle shows that divisive people create change. If you want to be a part of racial progress, you may very well have to become a master at polarization. A perfect example of a master polarizer is white America's favorite Black freedom fighter: Dr. King.

It's untrue that Dr. King was a unifying figure for America, as many white Americans believe and suggest. He was among the most polarizing figures of his time. The whole Civil Rights Movement was disruptive and divisive—that was the point of it all. In preparation for the famous Birmingham Campaign, King explained that he and other Civil Rights activists—including Ralph Abernathy, Dorothy Cotton, and James Bevel—planned to "create a situation so crisis-packed," it could bring the whole city to a halt.[4] In February 1968, a Harris poll indicated that Dr. King was the most hated man in America, which is why he was murdered in cold blood by a white supremacist only two months later.[5]

In his book *Blueprint for Revolution,* Serbian revolutionary Srdja Popovic recounts an early meeting with Syrian activists who were working to depose the dictator Bashar Hafez al-Assad. In the 1990s, Srdja and a group of comrades organized to oust Serbian dictator Slobodan Milošević, the notorious "Butcher of the Balkans," through creative, nonviolent campaigns. What began as a series of hilarious pranks pulled by a handful of college students evolved over a decade into a movement of seventy thousand Serbs who pressured the dictator to step down. Since then, Popovic and his colleagues have founded the Center for Applied Nonviolent Actions and Strategies (CANVAS) and trained activists around the world in the craft of civil resistance. That's why the Syrian activists wanted to meet with them.

At the meeting, one of the Syrian activists made a comment about roughing up the dictator, and an argument erupted, with another activist expressing her exhaustion with violence. Slobodan Đinović, one of the CANVAS organizers, asked the woman, "What are you here for?"

"I'm here to learn how to replace Assad through peace, not through war . . ." she responded. "We've had enough war."

Đinović agreed violence wasn't the way to depose Assad, but he wanted to correct something else she said. "I can tell you have good intentions," he answered. "And because you're here, I can tell that you are very, very courageous. But you have to understand that we are here to plan a war."[6]

The Syrian activists were puzzled. They had come there to participate in nonviolent struggle, and this man was over here talking about war.

"Being nonviolent doesn't mean you're not fighting hard," he explained. "You just fight with other means."[*]

This story perfectly illustrates a costly misconception about nonviolent struggle. Too many people think nonviolent struggle is inoffensive, docile, and nonconfrontational. They think protest is done right when everyone is happy with it. They think the "civil" in civil disobedience means "polite." But real nonviolent

---

[*] I want to spell this out because it can be confusing to people who haven't studied nonviolent struggle. Many practitioners call nonviolent struggle "war without weapons." So when he says they're there to plan a war, he's alluding to a militant approach to nonviolence.

struggle is nothing of the sort. Nonviolence is confrontational in opposing oppressors and aiming to cripple oppressive systems. Because nonviolent struggle seeks to disrupt the status quo, it is infuriating to those who are committed to the current oppressive order.

This is why it's inappropriate to call nonviolent actions "peaceful protests." As I hinted when I wrote about my last lunch with the Stones, nonviolent freedom fighters aim to disturb the peace until there's justice.

Nonviolent struggle is based on what some call "the social view of power." In a nutshell, this view suggests that the status quo depends on the mass cooperation, or consent, of the general population. "By themselves," writes Gene Sharp, "rulers cannot collect taxes, enforce repressive laws and regulations, keep trains running on time, prepare national budgets, direct traffic, manage ports, print money, repair roads, keep markets supplied with food, make steel, build rockets, train the police and army, issue postage stamps or even milk a cow. People provide these services to the ruler through a variety of organizations and institutions. If people would stop providing these skills, the ruler could not rule."[7]

From there, the logic flows that if people were to withdraw their consent through actions like boycotts and strikes, they could weaponize that power to compel authorities to meet their demands for justice. The Civil Rights Movement in the U.S. is a testament to that theory of power in practice. Through boycotts, freedom rides, marches, sit-ins, and other acts of civil disobedience, Civil Rights activists intentionally wielded power over and against the white supremacist structure of American society.

They found ways to make the cost of upholding racism more expensive—whether socially or financially—than the cost of granting the movement's demands. And they pissed off a bunch of people in the process, causing social unrest throughout the American South.

Fortunately, social movements only need about half the population to agree with them, and far less of the population to actively participate in them.* As I mentioned before, the research on nonviolent movements has revealed that a skilled minority in sustained nonviolent resistance can run colonizers out of a nation, topple dictatorships, and compel governments to repeal racist laws. This truth can protect us when white people try to tone police us in the name of unity.

In their book *This Is an Uprising*, movement historians Mark and Paul Engler argue that polarization is essential to effective nonviolent movements for social progress: "By taking an issue that is hidden from common view and putting it at the center of public debate, disruptive protest forces observers to decide which side they are on."[8] When the Freedom Riders performed their own illegal integrated bus rides and the national press published news of the violent mobs who attacked them for it, white Americans had to face the question: are you on the side of your neighbors trying to peacefully ride the bus or on the side of the

---

* I learned this in a nonviolence training. According to Momentum Community, a movement training center and incubator, movements are more likely to succeed when they have "passive popular support," meaning 50 percent of the public agrees with them. This is in addition to what we call "active popular support"; that's the 3.5 percent of the public that actually engages in sustained nonviolent action campaigns.

vicious mob attacking them? Once people have chosen a side, they're more likely to take action that's consistent with their position. Polarization can be crucial to a winning strategy.

This doesn't mean we should just throw unity out the window altogether. A certain kind of unity is important. We do need to be united for the purpose of jamming the gears of the white power structure through nonviolent struggle. We need unity in our vision of tomorrow, unity in what strategies we'll use to realize that vision, and unity in what values will guide our work as we fight. But we don't need the fetish for the idea of racial harmony that's so popular in white America. We seek unity not for its own sake but for a purpose.

When Dr. King talked about people coming together in his "I Have a Dream" speech, it was for the purpose of engaging in disruptive nonviolent campaigns. He says, "With this faith we will be able to work together, to pray together, to struggle together, to go to jail together, to stand up for freedom together, knowing that we will be free one day." White people are out here quoting the "together" part and leaving out the part about "struggling" and "going to jail."

To see what "unity for struggle" looks like in practice, let's stick with one the most famous protests Dr. King was involved in: the Montgomery Bus Boycott. Unity played a central role in the success of that campaign. Ninety percent of Montgomery's Black citizens stopped riding the bus. They also organized a carpool to get protesters to and from work. And their unified actions dealt a major blow to systemic racism, as the U.S. Supreme Court ruled racial discrimination in public transportation unconstitutional. That's unity for struggle in action. It's important to note that the success of the Montgomery Bus Boycott didn't depend on convincing white people to "come to the table" and sing "Kumbaya." The Black community needed unity among themselves, so they could act collectively.

The same is true in all struggles for social progress. We primarily need unity with those who are working toward the same goal.

The apocalypse taught me the truth about unity: that unity isn't possible, necessary, or even desirable with everyone. We actually don't want unity with our oppressors. We want freedom.

There may be some sort of Beloved Community in humanity's future, but if such an arrangement of love and togetherness will ever exist, it lies on the other side of a sustained struggle against white supremacist power. Which means that, for now, the kind of unity we need is the unity for struggle. I mean a struggle against white supremacy that is based on wise, broad, strategic plans to disrupt the flow of racist power, to replace inequitable structures with equitable ones, and to make racial justice our common sense. I mean mobilizing a critical mass of nonviolent actors to stay in the struggle until victory is won.

Popular, superficial notions of unity undermine the genuine unity movements need to succeed, because they saddle us with goals that can't be achieved. When people assume everyone is needed to create change, they preoccupy themselves with moving immovable people or trying to bring unity between groups who have fundamentally different political desires. That's a fool's errand. The unity we need to prioritize isn't among our opponents but among those who share our values.

It may sound counterintuitive. Why would we need to build

unity among people who already agree with one another? But when you realize that the fight for racial justice is less about expressing the same values and more about taking concerted action, it begins to make more sense. Millions of people can believe that racism is a problem, but it doesn't mean they agree on how to go about solving it. Concerted action requires unity on what strategies will be used in our struggle. Are we using nonviolent strategy or taking up arms? Are we focusing on poverty or police brutality? Are we willing to work with police or not? Will we build a multiracial or all-Black coalition? Unity must be built on questions like those. And building that kind of unity is a big enough challenge to require all of the energy of those who want to organize a revolution against racism.

In fact, disunity among activists is one of the biggest obstacles facing movements for racial justice today.

Nothing impedes the work like infighting among activists. A heartbreaking example comes to mind when I think of this.

I was invited to a march in downtown Los Angeles in the summer of 2020 by an organizer we'll call Ahmad. When I caught up to the protest, I saw Ahmad with the megaphone in his hand, as per usual, leading chants. But marching next to him was a taller guy in a stylish hat with a megaphone of his own, chanting something different. Marchers looked around at each other with confused looks on their faces, not knowing what we were trying to say to the public.

But that was the least of our problems. Before long, Ahmad and hat guy started shoving each other. The march fell apart as the crowd worked to de-escalate the situation.

"Okay," Ahmad finally announced. "All my people are gonna regroup at City Hall."

"Your people," yelled one of the protestors. "There is no '*your* people.' It's all of us!"

That argument ignited a whole new argument, involving more protesters than before.

Finally, another organizer was able to get Ahmad to calm down and leave the march. I left, too.

I tell that story to illustrate how easily infighting can literally stop the work of the movement. The activists that day couldn't even agree on what their message was, and it derailed their action. I think that scene is symbolic of all the ways that decisive action for racial progress can get derailed by disunity.

I've seen my fair share of racial justice work derailed when people quarrel over who gets the megaphone, whose politics are better, and who has the right to organize in what neighborhood. I've had to talk a seasoned activist down from punching a new activist in the face at an action because of old beef. More than once I've talked with different groups about building coalitions, only to find out this group can't work with that group because so-and-so fell out with so-and-so years ago and they haven't figured out how to patch things up—or don't want to.

I'm not saying any or all of these divisions are frivolous. But I wonder how silly it must look to the powers that be, to see people saying they want to change the world but can't find enough unity to walk down a street together. I think of how weak we are when we're fighting each other.

We need to take unity for struggle as seriously as our opponents do. In her book *We Will Not Cancel Us,* author and movement veteran adrienne maree brown makes a serious point about all the infighting we do in movement space that has stuck with me: Big Brother is studying our fights.[9]

The powers that be have always watched our movements closely to see what divisions they can exploit. In the 1960s and 1970s, the FBI's Counterintelligence Program (COINTELPRO), for example, exacerbated known internal divisions among the Black Panthers, as well as tensions between the Panthers and other groups, to weaken the Black freedom movement. They would forge an insulting letter to an activist in the name of someone else in the movement they had beef with, and they infiltrated the Panthers with undercover agents to stir up conflict. They were determined to prevent unity in the movement because they understood how important it is for struggle.

In our highly surveilled context, it's even easier for those who want to prevent racial progress to monitor and dismantle our movements, especially when we do the work for them by posting our conflicts, disagreements, and misunderstandings on social media or fight with each other in the middle of the streets. We're telling our opponents exactly where our pressure points are. This doesn't mean conflicts among activists should never happen or that callouts are never appropriate. I'm saying that we should be just as determined to build and maintain healthy community as our opponents are determined to destroy it.

So the truth about unity is that we need to be preoccupied with unity for struggle. It is the only type of unity relevant to racial justice conversations right now. I keep emphasizing the struggle part because so many people are trying to bypass the conflicts that are necessary to get to harmony. Oftentimes, to make peace, we have to stir up a little trouble. Every person we revere as a paragon of justice advocacy has recognized this.

Frederick Douglass once wrote, "Those who profess to favor freedom and yet depreciate agitation, are people who want crops without ploughing the ground."[10] After the Montgomery Bus Boycott, Dr. Martin Luther King Jr. admonished his congregation to keep struggling, saying, "Freedom only comes through persistent revolt, through persistent agitation, through persistently rising up against the system of evil. The bus protest is just the beginning."[11] Alicia Garza, a Black Lives Matter co-founder, writes: "Every successful social movement in this country's history has used disruption as a strategy to fight for social change. Whether it was the Boston Tea Party to the sit-ins at lunch counters throughout the South, no change has been won without disruptive action."[12] If this has been true throughout our history, what reasons do we have to think that racism today will end through any other means?

I'm tired of people offering empty sentiments, religious platitudes, and superficial gestures of unity to a problem that is taking lives every day. Racial progress has never been given freely to any generation before us. It has always been hard-won. I fear people spit on the graves of those who gave their lives for freedom by suggesting racial progress is as easy as a few conversations and hugs. The only thing that will end racism is struggle.

12

Building Our Own Tables

These were angry tears. After only three months in my dream job at *Relevant,* I'd determined the racial stress was too much. After that meeting, I broke down and promised myself I'd quit after finishing my first year at the company.

Hours earlier, the editorial team had gathered in the bullpen for our weekly content meeting. This meeting included the CEO, the brand manager, and everyone from the editorial team I managed: the senior writer, copy editor, editorial assistant, and contributing editor. The purpose of the weekly content meeting was to discuss what articles would be published on the website the following week and to collaborate on headlines. When they hired me as managing editor, the content schedule was mine to fill. Each week I was asked to present twenty new articles I'd chosen for publication.

I'd developed some mechanisms to make the task of reading, curating, and editing eighty articles per month more manageable. One of those mechanisms was to use the calendar and public holidays to generate ideas. I'd reached out to indigenous writers to publish during Native American Heritage Month in November, to therapists who could write about navigating family conflict for the holiday season, to pastors for articles about Advent, and so on.

The content wasn't always serious. I published some fun articles as well, like "The Definitive Ranking of Thanksgiving Sides." There were no complaints about that approach until that day in January, when the leadership realized that I'd be using the same approach for Black History Month.

"Wait," said the CEO. "We're going to publish something every day for Black History Month?"

"Yes," I answered.

"Well, no one talked to me about it," he complained.

I didn't know how to respond. For three months, I'd done exactly what I'd been trained to do: "fill this calendar." I replied that I was unaware the CEO expected me to ask his permission every time I was planning future content, since that's what he'd hired me to do. The company leaders had never established a protocol that I would ask permission to post articles related to a national commemorative season like Black History Month.

His lip curled as he scrolled through February's twenty-eight days on the computer screen. "What about people who aren't interested in that?"

I answered that we'd already been doing the same thing for other commemorative seasons. I figured we'd continue to do that for Black History Month, Women's History Month after that, and the other commemorative seasons after that as well.

"Oh! So you're just making decisions now," he said. My subordinates froze, and carefully made "Did he really just say that?" eyes at me for a second. I didn't know how to respond either.

I wanted to be respectful. And I couldn't think of a respectful way to say, "Well, that's what you hired me to do, isn't it?"

So I bit my tongue.

He went on about how we would "need to be careful not to waste editorial energy" and complained that "now we'll have to post seven or eight articles per day" to offset posting one related to race for Black history.

When I began to push back as gently as I could a couple minutes into his monologue, the boss stormed out of the meeting. That was the end of the discussion, the end of the Black History Month project, and the beginning of the end of my tenure as a *Relevant* employee.

Soon after that meeting, I was stripped of all decision-making power. I remained managing editor in title, but oversight of web content was given to the brand manager, oversight of magazine content was delegated to our contributing editor, and final say on video content was assumed by the CEO. My role became that of an individual contributor and on-camera/on-air talent. There was no meeting with me to explain any of this.

I spent the next six months feeling like a token. In the end, I wouldn't make it a year. I would quit that summer, largely because of race fatigue. I packed my little Kia Rio and headed back to Los Angeles.

I tell this story about *Relevant* to illustrate a fatal flaw of many predominantly white institutions, something I'll expound on in this chapter: namely, that they prioritize racial diversity over racial equity. White institutions are often far more interested in appearing nonracist than in sharing real institutional power or intentionally considering, much less serving, Black people's interests. All of this means Black people may need to rethink the fight for the proverbial seat at the table in white institutions. We need tables of our own.

There are some hard pills to swallow about working in predominantly white institutions, especially for Black people who hope to reform them. The first is that many of the leaders in these institutions are terrified of racial reform. That's because the white imagination often envisions racial reform will bring its institution to ruin—like when the CEO of *Relevant* imagined some digital one-drop rule where publishing one racial justice article a day, twenty-eight days out of the year, would lead to "wasted" editorial energy and a decline in website clicks. There's a perceived cost to being seen as concerned with the interests of Black people. White businesses fear losing white customers, many white politicians fear losing white voters, and many white churches fear losing white parishioners unless they serve their needs exclusively. So, as policy, they make it their business to serve white people at the expense of others.

The second hard pill is tethered to the first. It's that white institutions have an immune system that seeks out and expels personnel who threaten to upset the racial order within the org. In that way, they can rid themselves of the terrifying prospect of racial reform before it has a chance to spread.

In hindsight, it seems to me that the *Relevant* CEO put me through what sociologist Glenn Bracey calls a "race test." Bracey's argument stands on the premise that white institutional space is established first and foremost to serve the interests of "white people." This commitment to centering the needs and desires of so-called white people can influence everything from the musical genres on the office playlist and what behavior and styles of dress are considered "professional" to who gets promoted and what products are likely to be greenlighted.

Bracey explains that a race test happens when white people perform racial microaggressions on Black and brown people in their organization to assess how committed Black people and people of color are to maintaining and securing the priorities of so-called whites. In his study of seven white-led churches, Bracey identified two broad categories of race tests. It's important to note that the foundation of Bracey's argument is that white churches are ultimately white institutional space, just like any other predominantly white institution. So what applies to the churches in this study also applies to nonreligious institutions.

First, there is the "utility-based" race test. He writes, "These forms of race tests appeared in the form of an exaggerated welcome for potential congregants of color. The catch, however, was that the welcome was based on newcomers' racial status and their willingness to use that status to serve . . . perceived racial needs while not challenging the normative boundaries of white privilege and power within the space."[1] This helps explain why Black people are so often hired by white-led organizations but disempowered, even when appointed to positions of leadership. At *Relevant,* my exaggerated welcome was the offer to become the managing editor, when what they really seemed to want was a cool-looking Black guy to bolster their nonracist image in their daily video content.

The second kind of test Bracey identifies is the "exclusionary race test." He tells the story of attending a church event in a predominantly white, working-class neighborhood that was organized to welcome him to the congregation and introduce him to other church members. Attendees were asked to introduce themselves with an interesting fact about themselves. When the first person responded to the prompt by sharing the name of his favorite gun, it became the theme of the introductions. Bracey describes what happened when the leader of the Bible study finally stepped up:

> "I don't know what the real name of my favorite gun is . . ."
> —[he] cocked an imaginary gun and pointed it at me and the Latino first-timer next to me—"I call it my 'China Gun' because when I shoot it, it just goes 'C***k! C***k! C***k! C***k!'" With each "C***k," [the leader] drew back with mock recoil and aimed at us again.°

Bracey explains that if he hadn't been conducting research, he would've left the Bible study after the "China Gun" comments—which is the goal of exclusionary race tests, to compel nonwhite people to leave by creating a hostile environment.

I see the content meeting about my Black History Month project as one of many race tests at *Relevant*. The CEO's question "What about people who aren't interested in that?" wasn't the same as cocking an invisible gun and shooting at me, but his implication that Black history was of little interest to most peo-

---

° The word I've censored is an anti-Chinese racial slur. Since I don't belong to the group this slur has been used against, I've decided to censor it, just as I would want non-Black people to treat anti-Black racial slurs.

ple invoked a history of indifference to Black life and suffering that has always been a package deal with anti-Black violence. Black suffering couldn't be so pervasive and consistent without the indifference and contempt of so many white organizations. And from where I sit today, scoffing "So you're just making decisions now" in front of my team looks like a public attempt to put an "uppity Negro" in his place. I suppose I was expected to prove my loyalty to white comfort by saying I care about people who don't care about Black history or apologizing for exercising authority I was given, but I wouldn't.

Once I "threatened the boundaries of white institutional space," the senior leadership kept rearranging the editorial department in ways that left me feeling disempowered. In the weeks leading up to my departure, I kept saying to my Black co-workers, all two of them, "It feels like they want me to quit." They agreed that it seemed that way—and it worked.

I say all of this for the benefit of my beloved Black siblings struggling to thrive in institutions that were never made for you. You probably aren't hallucinating if you feel like you entered an org that seemed excited to have you because you are Black and then seems to punish and marginalize you for that very same reason. It happens all the time. I don't think people who believe they're white always know that they're acting as white blood cells in a body where anti-Blackness is homeostasis. I don't think anyone at *Relevant* *meant* to contribute to a racially insensitive environment, not even the CEO.* But intentions and impact aren't always the same thing.

---

* In fact, all of the company leadership, including the CEO, reached out to apologize, listened to my suggestions for changes to be made by the company, and even tried to implement some of them later.

To those who feel compelled to fight for reform in those spaces, I respect that decision, even though I don't share the same faith that reform is always possible. But I think it would serve you to know that many of these places are so slow at changing because they don't want to be changed.

Meanwhile, to the world outside their walls, white-led institutions do their damnedest to present a nonracist image without doing anything to actively organize themselves against mainstream white power. The irony is that many of them use racist tactics to build and uphold the facade.

When I published my experience at *Relevant* in a viral Medium blog post a year later, a former *Relevant* employee reported that—sometime before I worked there—the company asked some of its white writers to use "ethnic-sounding" pen names on several articles they'd written. The instruction to delve into digital Blackface was meant to give the company a veneer of racial diversity. Somehow, pretending to be diverse seemed a more viable option than recruiting more Black people, indigenous people, and people of color to write for them. Other companies may not use such extreme measures, but they have their own ways of putting on their best nonracist makeup. And even when it's well intended, signaling to the public that one's company values racial diversity won't save the next George Floyd.

This is an important point to make, because a ton of commercial institutions showed symbolic support for the Black Lives Matter movement in the summer of 2020, but their commitment to structural change remains to be seen. At a time when people from Dallas to Amsterdam were chanting "Black Lives

Matter," many companies apparently wanted to *be seen* singing along. "Black lives matter: Amazon stands in solidarity with the Black community," read the home screen of Amazon's Fire TV. Nickelodeon interrupted their regular programming with 8 minutes and 46 seconds of silence to represent the amount of time George Floyd lay pinned to the ground by Derek Chauvin's knee, struggling for breath.[*] Viacom, Comcast, Starbucks, Google, and others made similar statements.

And yet, by the end of the year, diversity recruiter April Curley was fired from Google after enduring what she described as years of racial hostility, including being told her thick Baltimore accent was a disability.[2] Respected computer scientist Timnit Gebru was also fired from Google after publishing a paper that called out racism in big tech.[3] In early 2021, diversity managers at Amazon disclosed to *Recode* that Black employees are "promoted less frequently and are rated more harshly than non-Black peers," a fact also backed by the company's internal data.[4]

As nice as it was to see the gestures of support from big business that summer, many of these corporations, a year after the killing of George Floyd, had yet to put their money where their Black Lives Matter tweets were. On the anniversary of George Floyd's killing, Michael Harriot reported for *The Root* that American corporations had donated less than 1 percent of the $50 billion promised into any specific antiracism reform. If corporations, educational institutions, religious organizations, and nonprofits don't change the racist cultures and institutional structures that make them hostile environments for Black peo-

---

[*] It was later revealed that George Floyd was pinned to the ground for 9 minutes and 29 seconds.

ple, they'll prove that their Black Lives Matter statements from 2020 were little more than institutional virtue signaling.

My time at *Relevant* highlighted the apocalyptic lesson that an institution is either actively working against the anti-Black gravity of the white world, or it's anchored by it.

Anti-Blackness is like an accent people pick up even if they don't immediately recognize it as such. In order to "hear" their anti-Black accents, people must depend on the feedback of trusted Black people to point it out. And changing an accent requires active listening to those you wish to communicate with as well as to yourself. You practice, slowly and deliberately, to change your speech.

The fact that anti-Blackness is everywhere means that an organization can't be defensive about racism if it wants to be antiracist—even if it's working on the problem. Organizations that want to be antiracist will make reassuring Black people of their efforts a priority. When their behavior invites critique, they say, "Yes. Anti-Blackness has been a problem here. We're sorry. We're working on it. Here's how. . . ."

Antiracist institutions also don't conflate the presence of antiracists within their organization with being an antiracist organization. Having a diversity, inclusion, and equity employee you won't listen to—or some kind of racial justice department or center you barely cross paths with—isn't the same as having an org-wide antiracist ethos and practice. Until an institution is actively investigating and confronting white supremacy within the organization, it's a racist institution.

Real antiracism is tangible. It includes things like buy-in from senior leadership, efforts to educate staff and leaders, accountability for racist behavior, explicit inclusion of antiracism in the core values of the institution, and incorporation of Black people and people of color in positions of real institutional power.

Because institutions have such tremendous power to uphold or dismantle the status quo, it's crucial that they find the moral courage, social imagination, and political will to actively engage in the ongoing antiracist revolution.

Institutions are essential for racial progress because they channel and even strengthen our collective power. Nonviolent strategists use a framework called "pillars of support" to illustrate this idea. Picture a structure like an ancient Greek temple with large columns holding up the roof. The roof of that temple represents the social problem a movement is trying to confront—in this case, racism. The columns represent all the institutions and social blocs that uphold that social problem: like, the police and military, the educational system, the media, organized religion, and government. These institutions, more or less, are the means by which the general public lends its power to the status quo.

Skilled freedom fighters learn to analyze the pillars of support, to determine which ones depend on the mass participation of ordinary people and are therefore vulnerable to pressure from campaigns of mass defiance. For example, they might ask: can the security forces in a totalitarian regime be convinced to ignore orders from the dictator? If so, the dictator will lose the tanks and guns and other weapons that empower them to quell protests. (This happened in the Philippines in 1986, and it helped the People Power movement end the dictatorship of Ferdinand Marcos.) When the pillars that support the status quo begin to shift, change is on the horizon.

In the U.S., we have our own pillars of support. Our educational system supports the racist power structure by refusing to offer an accurate account of our racist history and also by funneling "misbehaving" students—especially Black girls, who get disciplined and expelled at a disproportionately high rate—through the juvenile justice system. Evangelical churches support the racist status quo by refusing to address racial justice issues or, in many cases, supporting white supremacist officials like President Trump. The media supports the racist status quo by overrepresenting Black and brown people as criminals on the evening news and uncritically publishing police press releases in their stories. The list goes on. People working in institutions that support the white power structure need to be persuaded or compelled to stop cooperating with racism.

But bringing the roof down on racism isn't enough. We need alternative institutions to replace them. As I've written before, many people lack the imagination to envision what the world can look like without its current systems of injustice. This is why the first thing anyone says when you say "abolish prisons" or "defund the police" is, "Well, what else are we gonna do?" Without an alternative, people tend to default to the known status quo, regardless of how terrible. We can't just scratch our heads at the question "What will we do?" We need to experiment.

Thankfully, on the issue of public safety, experiments are already happening around the world. Some schools in the U.S. are experimenting with restorative justice circles instead of more punitive measures like detentions and suspensions, which are usually gateways to the prison system.[5] The incarceration rate in the Netherlands has halved since 2004, enabling them to close multiple prisons, because their model for mental health rehabilitation is proving more effective.[6] Finland is fighting recidivism by offering unhoused people a permanent, stable home, which has also nearly cut the number of long-term unhoused people in half.[7] With creativity and the courage to take risks, we can create new and better systems to address the social issues that police and prisons will never solve.

So what happens to our current institutions in the meantime? Do we all abandon them today and start building new ones? That's not realistic or reasonable. While some of us work on building the institutions of tomorrow, I still think there's value for others to seek to influence existing institutions. The slow pace of institutional change and the politicking required to keep it moving have often left me cynical about working within them. However, there's something to be said about the resources and influence that already exist in some established institutions. If those resources can be mobilized for racial justice, they could become powerful sources of legitimacy and support for the movement. Having advocates in these institutions is important.

But the major lesson I pulled from my experiences in institutions like *Relevant* is that we need to invest in Black-led institutions and institutions led by people of color, where the organizations' leaders have already adopted an explicit anti-oppression culture. We need institutions that center the needs and interests of oppressed people, institutions that intentionally work against norms of the white supremacist culture that envelops us and toward the antiracist world we aspire to live in.

Since leaving that company, I've only worked for organizations that are explicitly antiracist and led by justice-oriented Black people or people of color. The difference in my satisfaction at work has been incredible. No longer do I argue with my bosses about doing something as simple and obvious as posting articles about race during Black History Month. The teams I work with are challenging the hierarchical structures we encountered in white institutions, experimenting with more horizontal leadership structures. There are still challenges working among Black- and POC-led organizations, but I'm experiencing none of the racial stress I did as a token in predominantly white institutions.

Building Black-led institutions can provide a power base from which our people can work. If we spend all of our time and energy trying to persuade white people to lead their institutions differently but no time building our own institutions, we're left in the beggar's position, and white people will have no incentive other than conscience to share power with us. The white power structure could deny us the dignity and consideration we deserve, knowing we literally have no alternative. But if we build our own strong institutions, we can leverage their power to compel white power holders to meet our demands for a more equal society.

White people need to learn to share power. But we also need to empower ourselves. If we build our own tables, we will no longer have to beg for a seat at theirs.

13

How Black Love Became
Important to Me

By the time I moved back to Los Angeles, I'd grown skeptical about the possibility of any positive relationship between Black and non-Black people. Years of uncomfortable exchanges had exposed the anti-Black values held by my non-Black friends. Though the Black Lives Matter apocalypse unveiled anti-Blackness in work colleagues, in classmates, and even among the white people I once called family, nothing raised the question of whether any conciliation can be made between Black and non-Black people like the dating scene.

There was a time when race never would've been a factor in choosing a partner. But the more attention I paid to anti-Blackness in the world around me, the less comfortable I became dating non-Black women. In that season, the apocalypse would teach me the significance of Black love.

In late 2018, just before I moved back to L.A., my friend Lisa called me out of the blue to say she had feelings for me and wanted to know if I felt the same. She had a boyfriend, but she was testing the waters like someone who starts applying for jobs before quitting the one they already have (no judgment). I did have feelings for her, and she'd been one of my best friends. Nevertheless, I told her I wasn't comfortable "getting to know" someone who was in a relationship—not because I'm some model of integrity or because I thought it was wrong, I just didn't want to be the villain in their breakup story. But a few weeks after that conversation, she hit me up as a single woman, and we started "talking."

Lisa identified as Chinese American, and at one point I asked her how her family might react to someday meeting me if things got that serious. She said anyone she brought home would look something like me because she had a thing for Black men. But she also confessed that her dad had overcome some anti-Black prejudice in the recent past.

If I had known better at the time, I would've asked more questions about her "thing" for Black men. But the part about her father was unnerving enough. Does prejudice just go away? Or is it like a virus that goes dormant but can come back under stress? How would we know if her father was cured? I didn't want to be the test that revealed whether this man was completely free of Negrophobia, but I didn't ask any of these questions for fear of offense.

Lisa and I dated for a while, but the little cuts of being in an interracial relationship made it difficult to commit. I trusted her character and appreciated how supportive she could be, but from time to time, she would say something anti-Black that made me question if I wanted to risk having that kind of conversation again.

One time when we were talking about race, I mentioned how

non-Black immigrants can be anti-Black. "You can't say that," she responded, "because my parents are immigrants." She'd already told me that one of her parents had done intentional personal work to confront their anti-Black prejudices in the past, and we knew that her parent's anti-Black prejudices were consistent with a larger pattern of anti-Blackness in some Asian immigrant communities. Yet she started playing devil's advocate anyway. After going back and forth a bit, I lowered my voice and told her that some of the stuff she was saying sounded just like the things said by the white friends I couldn't keep. She admitted that she was offended for her folks, and that's why she'd gotten defensive.

Later in our relationship, we went out to a bar for Halloween. When a white woman passed by in a stereotypical "Native American" costume, I said facetiously, "I'm gonna ask that woman if she's indigenous."

Lisa pushed back. "I don't see why she can't wear it just because she's white."

For years now, indigenous people have been complaining about how a country that refuses to respect them and their lands has appropriated their culture and turned them into mascots. Lisa and I went back and forth debating, until she admitted she was already aware of the controversy and was just playing devil's advocate again.

These conflicts kept coming up. Another time, I gently let her know that something she said sounded anti-Black. She got upset and noticeably frustrated that I hadn't just given her the benefit of the doubt. "You know my character," she said.

Is this how it's going to be? I thought. I *did* know Lisa's character, but constantly sparring about race with someone I was dating was taxing. I'd already cut off other relationships—much closer ones—when people had done the exact same things.

My experiences with Lisa were a pattern in my relationships with non-Black women. I remember freezing in a late-night call with a white activist who said to me, "I see you talking about the problem a lot, but not the solutions. I can't be on the negative side of this thing." She didn't realize how many times I've explained to Instagram trolls that solving white supremacy isn't Black people's responsibility, any more than ending human trafficking is the responsibility of sex slaves. And explaining the same thing to a romantic interest wasn't my idea of a romantic evening.

Another white woman, while we walked down the sidewalk after a romantic night of singing karaoke, just randomly put her hand in my hair. *People!* I screamed inside. *We have literally written songs about not touching Black people's hair! Did she think the rules changed just because we were on a date?* In the moment, I chalked it up to ignorance and didn't say anything. But a week later, she brought it up. "Did you notice I touched your hair?" she asked. She said it with the look of a kid who has been caught stealing from a cookie jar. I threw up my hands internally. So she knew what she was doing!

A Middle Eastern woman I met on Tinder had a habit of saying "Nigga" with me on FaceTime. She explained that her ex-boyfriend, a Black man, told her she had her "Black card," and therefore could say "Nigga" all she wanted. *Nigga, no!* I yelled internally. But externally, I calmly explained to her that no, non-Black people don't get to use that word. If a man breaks into my house and tries to murder me with a crowbar, it's up to me whether I want to mount that crowbar above my fireplace and tell everyone the story or throw it away. But people don't get to come in my house and play with it. (All right, I know the police would take the crowbar as evidence, but you get what I'm saying.) It only took her a week to start playfully saying the N-word again.

The sad irony of anti-Blackness is that it can be performed by people who think they love and appreciate Black people, as in the examples above. All of these women claimed to have a preference for Black men, yet they would casually do and say things they knew were upsetting to Black people and then complain when they were called out on it. Too often, people who think they're nonracists mistake Negrophilia for genuine love. These types of experiences were feeding my general resentment toward non-Black people.

A few times, in my pre-apocalyptic life, I'd been the first Black man a non-Black woman had dated. They'd often say something like, "I never thought I'd go for a Black guy." Many times, I wanted to ask them, "Oh yeah? Who do you usually go for?" But I already knew the answer was often white guys.

The lie of human hierarchy has also shaped our beauty standards. It tells us that whiteness is more desirable and worthy of love. I'll never forget throwing a book on masculinity in the trash as I exited a subway train because the white male author kept talking about how all men aspire to woo a "golden-haired beauty." Those same Eurocentric messages often shape who many white women and non-Black women of color picture when they're imagining their Prince Charming.

The shadow side of Eurocentric beauty standards is a pervasive phenomenon of fetishizing Black bodies. It is widely known among Black Americans that many non-Black people are willing to date us or have sex with us but don't truly appreciate us. It's a dynamic so well known to Black people, HBO's *Insecure* explored it in its second season, when a Black male character named Lawrence is randomly picked up by two non-Black women at a grocery store. In the threesome sex scene that follows, the women inexplicably make the encounter racial, praising his "Black cock." But when he can't immediately go a second round, the women huff in disappointment: "What's the problem? We've been with a bunch of other Black guys who could come and keep going."[1] The two women immediately move on to discussing their dinner plans as they leave Lawrence in bed alone.

While this example was clearly scripted and contrived, it's an instance of art imitating a real-life dynamic. It evokes the memory of Jeannie Mai, a co-host on *The Real,* whose previous anti-Black comments resurfaced after she announced her engagement to the rapper Jeezy in an Instagram post in April 2020. In 2014, Mai came under fire for saying she "loved Black guys" but that she preferred to keep "dark meat on the side. White keeps me mean and lean, you know? That's why I married white. That's what I like."[2]

In late 2020, screenshots of a private conversation between white women went viral, in which they belittled Black men as smelly, easy, pathetic, and desperate.[3]

"Ill fuck with a blk guy even date for a bit but never marry," one commenter posted.

"Omggg sameee «rolling on the floor laughing emoji». I don't see the appeal," responded another.

"Black men would go above and beyond to please you cuz being with a white woman to them is a dream come true."*

They went on trading laughing emojis as they quipped about Black men being puppets who would let a white woman do anything to them. One of the most revolting of these comments scoffed about urinating in Black men's mouths, something they claimed white men would never allow, adding "Blk guys have low self esteem and love us." The spectacular thing about this particular story is that, after the screenshots went viral, some of the women involved insisted they weren't racists and were just expressing their "preference" for white men.

I'm not saying that all non-Black people behave like the women I've listed here or that they're all part of some secret anti-Black group chat. I'm saying that there's a spectrum of anti-Black antipathy that pervades white society, and it shows up in intimate relationships.

It's almost astounding how violently anti-Black non-Black people can be while claiming to not be racist or even to love Black people. As I navigated these relationships, wondering what compelled these non-Black women to want to be with me while doing things they knew to be offensive to Black men, a woman I once called a mentor helped me see some uncomfortable truths about this kind of behavior.

---

* This chapter alone could be its own book, so I can't cover these dynamics in an exhaustive way. But Frantz Fanon wrote about these dynamics—the racial politics that often make white men more desirable to women of color and white women desirable to Black men—in his book *Black Skin, White Masks*. Suffice to say that there's a lot going on psychologically and politically in interracial relationships.

Nasi was a professor at a local university and activist who special-
ized in Black radical literature. I met her at a protest and was so
impressed with her knowledge of Black political thinkers that I
wanted to learn everything she knew.

She identified as an Afropessimist, although she herself wasn't
Black. Afropessimism is an intellectual movement that takes the
fact that we live in the wake of the *Maafa* with the utmost seriousness. A major theme of this school of thought is that slavery
is more than an institution; rather, it is a relational dynamic that
endures today between Black and white people. To be clear: the
idea is that white people act the way they do because they
continue to see Black people as slaves and themselves as our
masters. Although I don't identify as an Afropessimist, some
Afropessimist thinkers have influenced my thoughts on racial
justice—thanks to Nasi.

Nasi and I would spend hours debating the most viable strategies for Black liberation. "You can't win a revolution through
nonviolence," she'd insist. She had studied the work of psychia-
trist and revolutionary Frantz Fanon and had become convinced
that Black people could only be free by taking up arms. I was
finishing up a course at the Harvard Kennedy School taught by
Srdja Popovic, a founder of the nonviolent revolution that ousted
Serbian dictator Slobodan Milošević, so I was obviously coming
from another angle. But while I never became convinced that a
violent revolution was the only way to remedy Black suffering, I
got a lot of useful insight from my conversations with Nasi. Perhaps the most disturbing, disheartening, and true of these in-

sights was the one that seemed to be showing up, albeit in microcosm, in my love life with non-Black women. Namely, that non-Black people engage in anti-Black violence because they enjoy it.

When the Afropessimist scholar Frank B. Wilderson III writes about the role of pleasure in anti-Black violence, he uses the French term *jouissance,* meaning "enjoyment, in terms of both rights and property, and of sexual orgasm."[4] *Jouissance* is a complicated term to unpack. It's like the pleasure of singing a song or eating a fully ripe mango, but in this context, it's getting that bliss from performing racial abuse.[*] In the same chapter, Wilderson invokes a phrase that the slaveholder Edwin Epps would repeat when he tortured his enslaved captives to illustrate this concept: "I am in my pleasure." Afropessimists argue that anti-Black violence is gratuitous—that is, it doesn't have to be the consequence of any kind of wrongdoing. Non-Black people don't have *reasons* for doing what they do to Black people. They do these things for the pleasure of it.

I don't want to overstate the harm done by common microaggressions by comparing them to the torture of enslaved people. The harm certainly isn't identical, especially not in the immediate aftermath. But *jouissance* helps describe the impulse of a non-Black woman who wants to say a historic and well-known racial slur to a Black man whom she knows is a racial justice advocate. Her desire to use the slur—or in Wilderson's terms, "transgress the prohibitions imposed on her enjoyment"—is the

---

[*] Wilderson is using language that has a very specific meaning to people familiar with the work of psychoanalyst Jacques Lacan. To go deeper in unpacking this term, I'd recommend looking up Lacan's work, but especially Wilderson's application of the idea to anti-Blackness.

only discernible source of her behavior. She says the N-word for the thrill of it.

Perhaps it sounds dramatic that little cuts could trigger such big thoughts. But the little cuts kill. As I wrote earlier, part of the problem with anti-Black violence is that white people and their accomplices only want to define racism by its most extreme and destructive forms. But psychologist and microaggression expert Gina Torino, who writes for the Center for Health Journalism, explains that "brief and commonplace daily verbal, behavioral, or environmental indignities, whether intentional or unintentional," have been correlated to higher levels of depression, trauma, suicidal ideation, heart attacks, and even early deaths in some communities of color.[5] Torino adds: "While individuals may not openly discriminate against people of color, they may engage in acts such as avoiding eye contact on the street or making assumptions about someone's intelligence or mental state. This subtler type of discrimination also negatively impacts health outcomes . . . described as 'death by a thousand cuts.'"[6]

This is why, in his book *How to Be an Antiracist*, Ibram X. Kendi writes: "I do not use 'microaggression' anymore. . . . A persistent daily low hum of racist abuse is not minor. I use the term 'abuse' because aggression is not as exacting a term. Abuse accurately describes the action and its effects on people: distress, anger, worry, depression, anxiety, pain, fatigue, and suicide."[7]

I was feeling some of those effects. By November, a lifetime of racial stress, including the microaggressions I've described on the dating scene, and reading a lot of Afropessimist literature had me in a crippling depression. *If anti-Blackness is everywhere, and the world depends too much on Black suffering to remedy it,* I thought, *why go on living?* At that point, I knew something had to change.

I told a friend about my struggle, and she introduced me to a therapist of color who helps people work through race-related stress. I needed to find some sustainable way to manage my anger at non-Black people. This anger was different from the constructive rage I felt at the white supremacist system. This anger made me want to cuss people out, punch my pillow when no one was around, and roll my eyes when non-Black people talked. And though Lisa and I were still seeing each other at the time, I felt alone because I didn't think I could talk openly and honestly about it with her.

I think Lisa could feel me pulling away. One day she said, "If you told me you needed to break up with me so you could find a Black partner, I would understand." We weren't a couple, so "breaking up" wouldn't have been necessary. But I should've just told her what I was going through. Whatever made her say that to me was prescient. I did need to find a Black partner— intentionally this time.

Around the time Lisa told me she'd respect me finding a Black partner, I kept running into Amber, a Black woman I'd known from my master's program. We knew each other through a mutual friend, and though I'd always thought she was beautiful, I never asked her out. Suddenly, she was everywhere. I'd see her at the coffee shop, pass her as I went to work, or run into her on my way to visit a friend. Finally, I asked her out, and she obliged.

Over tapas and drinks, I leaned in over the candle that separated us and asked with a smile: "So, how do you feel about building a Black ethnostate?" She chuckled: "I'm with it." *At last. Someone who gets it,* I sighed. She knew I was being facetious, but she also knew why the question was funny. We were both tired of the white world, but she was in a much better emotional state than I. She was sunshine enfleshed.

Before then, I'd dated Black women by happenstance. The fact that we were both Black hadn't been meaningful to me, but I did notice how other Black people responded when they saw me with my Black exes. "Black love," one woman exclaimed as I strolled with one of my exes down the street in Pasadena. In a grocery store, a woman once asked if she could snap a photo of one of my exes and me. Another time, while waiting in line at a dance club the bouncer whispered to me and a woman I was seeing: "I see what y'all doin', Black love."

For the next year, the brightest part of my day was when I got to see Amber. She'd often come to my apartment with a bottle of champagne, the most on-brand of drinks for her bubbly personality. We'd cook together, then I would lay my head in her lap and we'd share about our days before putting on something to watch. We'd go out to parties and own the dance floor with our moves we stole from Kid 'n Play's *House Party,* to the envy of other couples who only dreamed of being so in sync. We read bell hooks's "Understanding Patriarchy" together and would laugh about how problematic Booker T. Washington was as we cooked dinner. She became my very best friend. I had no idea two people could have so much fun in love.

What we never did was argue about race. There was no quibbling over microaggressions, no educating, no playing devil's advocate.

Finding Black love was awesome. 10 out of 10: would totally recommend.

On Instagram one day, a woman responded to my "Ask Me Anything" post by asking, "Would you ever partner with a white woman?"

"Probably not," I responded.

I got an angry DM in response. "What?! Why? You get that's like me saying I wouldn't marry a black [sic] man right? That's just crazy. . . ."

"It's actually not the same at all," I responded.

I stand by that response. It is not at all the same for Black people to think twice about partnering with non-Black people. Only someone who has no idea of the harm endured by Black people, even from their non-Black partners, would be able to say something like that.

Let no one convince you that racial politics resolve themselves automatically in love, sex, and romance. Beware the prophecies that predict that the coming "Browning of America" will save us from anti-Blackness. Unless we interrogate how our desires have been shaped by the social and political culture we live in—someone's "thing" for Black men, for example, or their "preference" for white women—the tensions between racial groups will play themselves out in our most intimate relationships.

Black people are wise to consider not dating non-Black people. It's a matter of safety, of ending the day in the arms of someone who knows exactly the type of hell you catch on a daily basis.

At the same time, I realize that Black love isn't always the most accessible to everyone. I also acknowledge that shared racial trauma doesn't automatically guarantee a healthy and happy relationship. For example, Black women may understand the struggles Black men have, but Black men will never fully understand the intersection of Black femininity. Therefore, while a Black man may breathe a sigh of relief to come home to a Black woman who "gets it," a Black woman may very well come home to sexist abuse from a Black man.

Nevertheless, the apocalypse made me come to the conclusion that Black love is important. Even if there are some caveats worth adding.

There are some who take all this information and conclude that if Black people don't choose a Black partner, it means they're not serious about Black liberation. I don't think that's always a fair conclusion. It's common to find Black activists who have non-Black partners. For some, race wasn't a factor in choosing a partner at the time they married. Others point out that white supremacist regimes once made interracial relationships illegal, making interracial love feel like a radical act of defiance for some. The marriage between iconic Asian American activist Grace Lee Boggs and Black Civil Rights activist James Boggs comes to mind, reminding me that interracial couples can be revolutionary. Each one has their reasons.

I especially don't think it's fair to be judgmental about Black women who partner with non-Black men. When I asked some of my Black women colleagues about these types of relationships, they explained that when Black women find non-Black partners, it's often because they've been overlooked by Black men, while Black men often choose non-Black women with the language of misogynoir dripping from our lips. Moreover, they explained, many Black women who marry non-Black partners still go hard for Black men in the struggle for justice anyway. So many variables factor into how people find partners—timing, proximity, and so much more—that it may be best to listen to people's love stories with curiosity rather than judgment. Perhaps it's most revolutionary to let Black people love whoever they want.

Nevertheless, I'd be remiss not to praise Black love. We can't talk about Black freedom in any comprehensive way without talking about Black love.

Black partnership is inherently subversive in a world that tells us we are undesirable and unworthy of love.

Black love is audacious in a world built to prevent us from self-love, that we would choose to love one another.

Black family is resistance in a world that fears Black people in groups.

Black partnership is reparations in a world where we were once forbidden to marry, where our families were systematically broken apart, and familial ties were regarded as for whites only. For all of these reasons, Black liberation is inherently tied to Black love.

So, no shade at all to those who have found love outside the race. But if Black love finds you, do your best to hold on to it.

14

To Fight or to Flee

"What's stopping you from buying a ticket to Jamaica right now?" my friend Tina asked. It was a good question. We'd just spent the last half hour talking about how I planned to spend 2020 traveling the world to see if I'd discover some other country I'd rather live in—one where the threat against Black bodies wasn't so great. But most of the countries I'd planned to visit had closed their borders to Americans because of the COVID-19 pandemic—all except Jamaica.

"I can't think of anything," I said. She was right. Nothing was stopping me from going.

"Sooo . . . are we doing this?"

"I—I guess so," I said with a nervous laugh.

I pulled up SkyScanner.com and found the cheapest one-way ticket to Montego Bay.

"I found a ticket for like $100," I told her.

"Are you gonna get it?"

"I just did."

"Yayyy! We're going to Jamaica," she cheered. After a moment, she said, "Wait. I just want to acknowledge what you did, in making a decision to choose yourself." She paused again. "I'm proud of you," she said.

Tina is a serious racial justice activist, but she's a huge proponent of Black joy and self-care. And in that moment, she was gently supporting me to find joy for myself and look after myself. Buying that ticket to Jamaica was the first step into my next apocalyptic lesson, a lesson about joy in the struggle.

It wasn't the first time I'd seriously considered expatriation. I first started imagining my life elsewhere during the 2016 election. I remember telling my friend Scott, a Black conservative Trump supporter, that if Trump won the election, I'd leave the country.

"You not goin' nowhere," he scoffed.

I rolled my eyes.

"Where you gonna go?" he said, calling my bluff. "Anywhere you go, you gonna have problems, and America is the greatest country in the world. If you leave the country, I'll put $10 toward your plane ticket."

But I wasn't bluffing. "My family isn't from here," I said. "And my older brother already left the U.S. for Abu Dhabi 'cause he just doesn't like it here." I was annoyed that Scott didn't seem to take me seriously.

Scott's line of reasoning is a common one. Some Black people talk as though America is all we have, as though access to Hulu and free refills at Chili's is worth all the mass shootings, police brutality, and predatory healthcare. I hated the assumption that all Black people who just happen to be on American soil have their roots so fixed here that they have no option but to take the heinous with the mediocre.

A few weeks after that exchange, I booked a six-city tour of Europe as a graduation present for myself. It gave me a taste of what life could look like away from the States, and it was gorgeous. The day and a half I spent in Amsterdam, I danced salsa in the middle of the street to a live band who'd blocked an intersection. In Rome, I ran into a Black former classmate in the Plaza del Popolo after singing Bob Marley's "Redemption Song" with a local busker. There was paella and people-watching on a beach in Barcelona, and even though I spent my only night in Paris hiding in an alleyway because I found a bedbug in my Airbnb, I'll never forget blurting out loud, "Damn this place is charming" when I first stepped out of the train station. And I'll never forgive my Uncle Leroy for depriving me of the chance to enjoy some authentic fish and chips when I visited him in London.

It'd be easy to assume that I felt freer in Europe because I was a tourist, unaware of the racial dynamics at play in the countries I visited. But I wasn't so oblivious. I didn't experience the depths of racial hierarchy as an American tourist abroad, but I was still paying attention. I noticed that most of the immigrants selling trinkets on Barcelona's boardwalk were dark-skinned. In Rome, out of a sea of pedestrians, I was the one who was "randomly" stopped and searched. I heard the way some people whispered about Muslims in Amsterdam.

And yet, with every city I visited, I could imagine myself having a happier life there.

I felt a little guilty about enjoying myself in Europe while my friends marched the streets for the slain in the States. But I never forgot the lesson of that trip: Black people need space for joy. That Black joy, in itself, is a profound rebellion in a world where anti-Black terror abounds. We deserve joy, not pain and struggle.

Ever since that trip, I'd daydreamed about leaving America for good. But the coronavirus pandemic turned that consideration into a decision. That and the threat of American fascism.

I don't know that I've seen anything in my lifetime that illustrates the crisis in American public leadership like the coronavirus pandemic. America led the world in COVID-19 cases in part because of inept politicians who wouldn't follow the science. Many of those leaders rose to power through white supremacist strategies, and their "leadership" ended up disproportionately harming Black people: for example, the governor of my home state, Brian Kemp, who, weeks after the whole world was talking about the spread of the virus through asymptomatic people, claimed he didn't know COVID-19 could be spread by the symptomless—hence his late decision to issue a statewide stay-at-home order.

I kept thinking about the forces that had brought him into power at that crucial moment. According to *The Atlanta Journal-Constitution*, Kemp stole the gubernatorial election from Stacey Abrams "by purging 1.4 million voters from the rolls, placing thousands of registrations on hold, and overseeing the closure or relocation of nearly half of the state's precincts and polling sites. The unstated goal . . . was to reduce the voting power of unfavorable constituencies: black people, poor people . . . others."[1] In his gubernatorial campaign, Kemp pulled from Trump's play-book, appealing to the fears white rural Georgians held about the state's changing racial demographics. He ran as a self-proclaimed "politically incorrect conservative" promising to "round up illegals and take 'em home" in his "big truck."[2] In a nutshell: racism made Georgians vulnerable to Brian Kemp's "leadership" and, by extension, coronavirus.

Adding to my itch to leave the country was, of course, the president. Also elected due to racism, his intentional downplaying of the pandemic cost hundreds of thousands of lives.

Then there were the anti-lockdown protests. It was infuriating to see crowds of white people take to the streets, some waving Confederate flags, some crying "Tyranny!," some wielding weapons, to protest the stay-at-home orders. *This is what mobilizes white America?* I thought to myself. They're ready to storm capitol buildings with guns because they want to eat inside at Dairy Queen Grill & Chill?

To add insult to injury, the police let them do it. We had watched—for years!—as Black people got shot for holding items police allegedly mistook for guns: cellphones, belt buckles, you name it. Yet these grown white men in militia gear could walk up to police with AR-15s and yell in officers' faces with no consequences: no pepper spray, no batons, no arrests.*

In the confines of my Los Angeles apartment, I decided I'd seen enough. I resolved that I'd leave the country at my first opportunity. When I asked myself if the election of a new president could convince me to stay in the U.S., I realized that it couldn't.

---

* Again, the point here isn't that police should beat protesters, but we know how they would've likely responded had the protesters been Black because we've seen police brutally attack Black Lives Matter protesters for years.

I also couldn't be certain that Trump would ever leave office in the first place. He was talking as though he intended to be president for life, and I took that threat seriously.[3]

In late 2019, I began seriously talking with friends about getting exit strategies together. "I don't want to end up stuck in the U.S.," I kept saying. But that's kind of what happened in 2020. While the U.S. didn't lock Americans within its borders, so much of the world closed its borders to U.S. residents in order to keep the virus out. The very thing I feared had come to pass. I felt trapped in the States while a growing fascist raincloud continued to spread across the horizon.

The last thing I expected in 2020 was an uprising. For years, people had been saying the Black Lives Matter movement was dead, because we hadn't been seeing massive protests that characterized the earlier years of the movement. Then came the deaths, in what felt like rapid succession: Ahmaud Arbery, Breonna Taylor, George Floyd. For five months, the whirlwind of the global Black Lives Matter uprising derailed my plan to flee the country. I'd been writing about and studying social movements for years, dreaming of being part of a global uprising against white supremacy. I couldn't leave just as it was getting started.

That June, I hit the streets of Pasadena with the local, unofficial Black Lives Matter chapter, armed with my experiences from the subversive liturgy and other organizing groups and my studies in nonviolent struggle. By then, my studies had gone way beyond my personal reading list: I had mentors who'd helped

topple dictators around the world to bounce ideas off of. I was
excited to bring all the insight I'd gleaned over the years to the
streets. The turnout for protests in the summer of 2020 was unlike anything I've experienced before: hundreds of people, of all
kinds of different backgrounds, full of antiracist zeal, chanting
with all their might, "Black Lives Matter!"

My favorite thing to do in the streets, whenever I was given
the mic or megaphone, was to lead crowds in a game of Simon
Says to demonstrate the social view of power. "The status quo
depends on our mass obedience," I'd shout. "Therefore, it can
be changed through our mass defiance. And to make sure you
never forget that, we're gonna play Simon Says.

"Simon says clap three times," I'd instruct.

The crowd would obey.

"Simon says say your first name."

They'd do as I say.

"Simon says pull your pants down!"

Every crowd would laugh.

After that, I'd ask them to identify who truly has the power to
keep the game going. "We do!" they'd exclaim. Then I'd affirm
they were right—that the status quo depends on their consent,
just like the Simon Says game depends on their obedience. I
taught that lesson everywhere I went because it's the truth at the
center of all nonviolent revolutions: ordinary people already
hold the power to disrupt the status quo and create a new normal.

I'm not gonna lie. Though I hate the fact that we have to be in
the streets, teaching about revolutions and organizing resistance
for racial justice made me come alive. It was my joy to serve

people in that way. And over the next few weeks, the fresh wave of global protests would challenge me to get the connection between joy and struggle down into my bones.

On this particular afternoon, no cars could get through the traffic light at Colorado Boulevard and Fair Oaks Avenue in Old Pasadena because a handful of Black folk, led by a preteen named Sebastian, were dancing to "Wobble" by V.I.C. in the middle of the intersection. We were surrounded by hundreds of non-Black protesters, holding signs that said things like GET YOUR KNEE OFF MY NECK, BREONNA TAYLOR, and BLACK LIVES MATTER.

I was in the center of this dance circle, trying to keep up: I knew all the steps, but I wasn't in my twenties anymore. The day was hot, and I was winded from the march from City Hall. But dancing is one of my favorite things in the world. (I used to have a reputation of being the last one on the dance floor at any party.) It's one of life's greatest joys to me. And one doesn't simply stop dancing when "Wobble" is on! So I was determined to dance until I couldn't.

While resting to catch my breath, it occurred to me that the formation blocking the intersection represented a picture of Black liberation my friend Nasi always talked about in our chats. At the perimeter of the circle, white and non-Black people of color stood, disrupting the flow of business-as-usual, ready to confront anti-Black violence so that the Black people in the center could experience joy, even briefly.

The white people there weren't asking us for antiracist learning resources or trying to absolve themselves of white guilt by apologizing to us on behalf of all white people. They weren't advising us on what strategies for protest would most appeal to their racist family members. When Professor Nasi and I used to debate Black liberation over mimosas, she'd always come back to the same conclusion about non-Black people: "We need to get out of the way," she'd insist. In symbolic action, her thesis seemed to play itself out on the street that day. The space those non-Black allies were giving us did feel liberating.

I lay down on the hot asphalt and breathed deep into my back, until I could feel my whole body rising and falling.

Soon, and perhaps predictably, the global freedom high would wane, sobered in the U.S. by Trump's authoritarian crackdown of the movement.

I thought I'd already seen enough of American history to be beyond the capacity for surprise, but I was stunned the day I watched federal agents in unmarked vehicles snatch antiracist protesters off the streets in Portland and New York, the latter in broad daylight.[4] I was equally appalled at the news from Kenosha, Wisconsin, that police allowed a white seventeen-year-old named Kyle Rittenhouse to troll the streets with his AR-15 rifle to "help businesses," according to his mom, before he fatally shot two Black Lives Matter demonstrators.[5] It recalled something my friend Mike had said: "When we see the police and the militia men march the streets together, we've gone full fascist." The Rittenhouse headline didn't fit Mike's description exactly, but it was too close for comfort.

As I watched the fascist counterrevolution unfold, my mind returned to something Srdja said to me in a conversation on my podcast. He described what he'd witnessed in Serbia as dictator Slobodan Milošević rose to power: two national wars, ethnic cleansing, hyperinflation, hundreds leaving the country (including his brother). "You see your world falling apart around you," he said, and added that he and his friends faced a choice: to fight or to flee.[6]

Srdja's description of the rise of authoritarianism in Serbia felt familiar, especially as Trump became more vocal about his intentions to undermine the 2020 election that summer.

A couple of weeks later, I landed in Montego Bay.

Tina did more than help me make the decision to leave the country. She also offered to come with me. She, too, wanted to escape America's special brand of anti-Blackness. I didn't see a reason to say no. She arrived in Mobay a few days before me and secured an Airbnb near Rose Hall.

At the end of our quarantine period, Tina and I started exploring the hot spots on the hip strip. It was kind of a ghost town since the pandemic had shut down the usual flow of tourists. We found a quaint little bar and marijuana dispensary right on the water with a gorgeous view of the Caribbean Sea, checked out live music on Thursday nights at a local lounge, and spent half days at Doctor's Cave Beach.

Doctor's Cave was one of our favorite spots. On a clear day, it's not just the gentle, clear waters that captivate the eye. It's also the lush mountains that jut out into the Caribbean Sea, the smell of jerk chicken wafting through the air from a nearby bar, and the sound of '90s reggae music spilling out onto the sand. Tina and I sat on towels just a few yards away from the water, shaded by a large red-and-white umbrella, she enjoying fresh coconut water and I a rum punch and festival. "Andre," she said, "it's been fourteen days, and I've yet to see a white person." She sighed. Tears flowed.

I could relate to her tears. I remembered a recent trip to a computer store to find an ethernet cable, where I got choked up when I looked around and realized no one was watching me. No one followed me with their eyes at the supermarket. No random stops and searches. I barely saw any police—and when I did, they didn't seem to notice me. They weren't interested in me at all.

I felt free. Free from the burden of proving I'm not up to something, or that I'm respectable. I felt free to just be.

I pushed my feet into the sand, completely burying them. Then I dug my hands in behind me until I'd made my own underground handles in the beach. And for the first time in my life, I felt energy from the earth gently massaging my hands and feet. The land seemed to greet me, pressing its body against mine like a house cat greeting its human.

That day on the beach in Mobay, without the static of white people chastising me, without the constant hum of headlines about hurt Black people, outside the reach of America's modern-day slave patrol, and unburdened by the duty to respond to the latest police killing, I found space to hear the world speak for the first time. It said "Welcome." And I was afraid. Was it okay for me to feel like the sand, and water, and sun were speaking to me? White Christianity had trained me to think that sort of conversation was forbidden. I looked out at the gorgeous blue hues massaging each other in the great expanse of Caribbean Sea— just water out there, as far as the eye can see. And I wondered how my ancestors felt when they first stood where I sat that day. They didn't call on white Jesus on that beach. I wondered if they felt how I felt, standing in front of that great expanse, if they felt like the world was speaking to them. I wondered what it said to them as they watched the *Maafa* pollute the air with colonial laws and slaveholder theology.

My cousin Delroy came to pick us up. He was our ride to go just about everywhere in Jamaica. Normally he worked as a tour guide, but with the pandemic having all but obliterated the tourism business, he had plenty of time to take us around.

Delroy's a barrel full of laughs and information about Jamaica's history. He's like a comedian and an encyclopedia wrapped into one. So, as per usual, we had a good laugh on the drive home from the beach. But I had a serious question on my mind.

"Do you think Jamaicans will accept me?" I asked as he dropped us off at our villa. I still had memories of feeling like an outsider on our visits when I was young.

"Wha yuh mean, mayne," he laughed. "You're Jamaican! Your mom from here. Your dad from here. You could be a citizen if you want!"

"Huh?"

"Yeah mahn! Yuh jus' to go immigration with your parents' birth paper and they'll give you your passport."

I had no idea I had citizenship rights by descent. But hearing my cousin, who'd been on the island his whole life, say it as simply as that—*You're Jamaican!*—warmed my heart. That news seemed to open a slew of possibilities for me. I got to planning in my head immediately. *If I gathered my papers,* I thought to myself, *I wouldn't have to leave the island.*

Duty called when I learned that a man named Anthony McClain had been shot in the back in my old neighborhood by Pasadena police. He was in the passenger side of a parked car when police approached the vehicle and asked him to step out. He took off running, kicking off his shoes as he ran.

I'd been strategizing with some activists in Pasadena remotely, but I felt survivor's guilt doing the work from the Caribbean. *They would come here for me*, I said to myself. *So I'm going to go back for them.* I was back on the streets in Los Angeles within days.

For two months, I submerged myself again in the work of the movement, but I also promised myself that while I was back in the States I'd get my papers together, pack up my apartment, and wait out election season in Montego Bay. If Trump won the election, I'd have whatever I didn't sell or throw away shipped to me in Jamaica.

Over those months, the static returned: the infighting activists eagerly competing for the title of Wokest of Them All; Trump blatantly announcing that he had no intention of leaving office; his sympathizers ramming their cars through protest lines; armed white militia groups threatening violence.

I also noticed a toxic work culture in one of the activist groups I was involved in. The group operated almost entirely on outrage, anger, and obligation, but I hadn't noticed until several weeks in. People were expected to comply with the whims of the lead organizer with blind obedience. And if people said they were tired, the leaders would give an impromptu speech about how our ancestors got tired but kept going. If people said they felt unprepared or unsafe doing an action, they'd get criticized for "operating out of fear." It burned a bunch of us out. And when I left the group, that same lead organizer started harassing me online and threatened to fight me if I ever came back to our old neighborhood.

My friends were concerned for my safety, since I often ended up on the frontlines of protests. "Do you have a bulletproof vest?" my friend Kristyn asked me, as I talked with her about my upcoming organizing plans. I didn't have one, and I didn't want to think I needed one. But the reality is that active shooter situations were seeming more likely after the Kyle Rittenhouse incident in August—especially since the president had praised him. Another friend solemnly encouraged me to prepare my last will and testament.

It all felt like too much. Sometimes I would just break down crying in my apartment. I had to broach the idea that I might actually die for the cause. I was willing to—but I didn't want to.

I became stressed to the point of constant exhaustion. I had trouble sleeping due to nightmares where different people—sometimes government agents, sometimes toxic organizing colleagues—kicked in my bedroom door and shot me in my sleep. But I kept pushing. *It's my duty,* I thought.

I founded a new activist group in Los Angeles and convinced them to stay off the streets until we'd gone through some nonviolent direct action training, which I paid for out of my own pocket. With so many potential threats emerging for protesters, the stakes were getting too high to hit the streets with passion alone.

I sought out training sessions that would prepare us for the kinds of munitions I saw the Los Angeles Sheriff's Department and Los Angeles Police Department using on protesters throughout the summer: tear gas, pepper spray, rubber bullets, the works. Someone put me in touch with an organization whose trainers had seen some of the most extreme scenarios I could imagine. I'm talking captured-and-tortured-by-secret-police-level resistance. And yet, the trainers told us that it was common and appropriate for people to decide what's an acceptable amount of risk for them. Not everyone decides they're arrestable. Not everyone decides they'll stick around when the tear gas comes out. We should respect each other's boundaries and support one another, because that's what healthy relationships look like—and in movements, healthy relationships matter.

The facilitator of that training walked us through exercises that would help us define safety for ourselves and build informed consent as we practiced civil resistance. And during one of the sessions, he said something to our group that I would never forget: "People are always talking about dying for the movement. Fuck that shit. I want you to live for the movement."

That statement—"I want you to live for the movement"—made me recall a promise to myself from years before that I wouldn't die like Dr. Martin Luther King Jr. According to the autopsy, Dr. King died with the heart of a sixty-year-old, even though he was only thirty-nine when he was assassinated. This is no doubt because of the constant stress and enormous pressure of his activism. It goes to show that having a literal big heart is not actually a good thing.

The struggle for Black freedom can engulf one's entire existence. I used to think that kind of life was admirable. I still believe that, but I've come to also believe it's unfair.

It's an injustice that some Black people would spend the majority of their lives and energy trying to clean up a mess they didn't make—that is, white supremacy. Some of us are compelled to do so, seeing it as an existential necessity, and wouldn't feel right in the world if we stopped. But it isn't all we want to do. Ask any Black activist to imagine that the entirety of the domination system, every -ism and phobia, had disappeared. What would they want to do with their lives?

I've asked several people this question. Sometimes their eyes pop open with glee. Others release a pregnant sigh or furrow their brows in deep consideration. The answers vary. We'd make more art, plant more gardens, take more trips, get more full nights of sleep, or just take more full weekends off—the list goes on. It's true that racism doesn't prevent us from writing songs or growing our own tomatoes, but it sure would help create more margin for pleasure and joy. Even Black Lives Matter co-founder Patrisse Cullors once tweeted that she doesn't just want to be "the Black Lives Matter girl." That resonated with me in such a deep way. We want to do more than fight for our lives. We want to live.

The apocalypse taught me that Blackness is more than suffering. In Blackness, there is joy and abundance. I don't want to work for justice solely from the trauma of living in the *Maafa's* wake. I want to live and rebel from a deep well of abundance, joy, hope, and righteous anger.

As much as I say that struggle is necessary for freedom, we must never forget that the reason we struggle is so that we can enjoy our lives. We must learn to create room for joy in the struggle. And there certainly are opportunities for that: it's those moments where you dance the Wobble in a blocked intersection, it's taking a day at the spa, it's throwing a barbecue with your movement friends. If there's one piece of advice I could give any new activist in this movement, it's not to take yourself too seriously. No matter how woke you get, it's important to schedule time to take naps and eat churros. Take mental health days. Find a hobby. Do something that brings you joy and do it regularly. Joy, like hope, makes the struggle sustainable. If you don't learn how to have fun while you fight the power, you're not gonna make it.

Joy doesn't just make activism more sustainable for individuals. It makes movements more powerful. I know lots of new activists want to be seen as serious revolutionaries—dressed in all black, armed with perfect politics, able to spell "All Cops Are Bastards" with their cigarette smoke. But joy is a movement's secret weapon.

When freedom fighters use joy, even humor, it can create problems for the powers that be. A creative protest at the southern U.S. border comes to mind. In 2019, artist and architecture professor Ronald Rael installed pink seesaws in the wall at the United States–Mexico border, to show the futility of building barriers. Kids on both sides of the border gleefully glided up and down at their new playground, a direct rebuttal to the divisive MAGA rhetoric about wall-building that was so popular at the time. This creative protest created a dilemma for authorities. If the Border Patrol had tear-gassed those kids as they seesawed on the border wall, they would have outraged the public and triggered protests. So they were forced to allow those kids to dance all over the anti-immigrant rhetoric of the Trump administration—which they also didn't want. This creative protest is an example of a dilemma action.

The powers that be know exactly what to do with a raging mob. Roll in the tanks. Launch the tear gas. Bring out the handcuffs. They will use your anger to vilify you and make you look threatening so that the resistance looks too dangerous and intimidating to join. All of that is harder to do when the resistance is having fun.

Dilemma actions are the bread and butter of nonviolent movements. When they're incorporated into strategic campaigns for clearly defined political objectives, they can compel oppressors to make decisions they'd rather avoid. The Civil Rights Movement was full of dilemma actions—among them, the lunch counter sit-ins and Freedom Rides—that forced white supremacists to expose their extremist violence to the rest of the nation and pull more people into the movement, ultimately winning Civil Rights legislation. I wouldn't describe the Civil Rights dilemma actions as joyful or humorous, but joy was still present in the movement. When optimism was high among Civil Rights activists for the end of racial segregation, activists from the Student Nonviolent Coordinating Committee described a kind of euphoria that would sometimes overtake them as they crossed arms with one another and sang together. They called that feeling "freedom high."[7]

Joy isn't always a part of dilemma actions, but joy definitely strengthens them. Serbian activists, for example, perfected a method for confronting the Milošević regime called "laughtivism," where they intentionally used humor to undermine fear of the dictator and attract more participants: they wanted the movement to be the coolest thing to do in town. And we've seen more strategic uses of humor in recent movements like Occupy Wall Street and Black Lives Matter.

Let's be real. Most people don't want to come to an angry party. There's a specific kind of person that responds to the call, "Something terrible happened! Let's go be mad about it in public together!" I am that kind of person, but I'm also one of the strangest people I know. Most don't want to risk their lives or go to jail, and shaming people for their lack of outrage or altruism isn't inspiring. Normal people are more likely to respond to a call to be a part of something fun. If you can show them a good time—and fighting the power can be a good time—well, that's an entirely different ballgame.

I decided that the movement may make a martyr of me someday, but I wouldn't kill myself for the cause. I booked a flight back to Montego Bay—departing just before the 2020 election—and resolved to get my affairs in order for whatever might happen next. Perhaps I'd return to the streets to fight for racial progress in Biden's America. Perhaps I'd stay in Jamaica or move someplace else. Either way, the idea was to get light enough to make a move.

I'd come so far from the days I used to lie on my stomach and draw pictures of the American Revolution. Now I felt more like a fugitive from white supremacy than an American patriot. Only time will tell where I find a place to rest, if that ever happens.

Before leaving, I gave away a bunch of books, donated clothes to Goodwill that I knew I wouldn't use, packed up my musical equipment, and sent my beat-up car to the junkyard. Then a few days before my departure, I dropped the boulder I'd once lugged around Los Angeles on the side of the road and bade it farewell.

15

Born Again

"Fi yuh muddah bloodline begin inna Westmoreland, wid a Scottish man name Pennycook an' one African woman weh name Bid'ah," my father explained through the phone. Before returning to Montego Bay, I had asked if we could exclusively "chat patois" from then on, thinking it would help me blend in with native Jamaicans. He obliged.

Chatting patois felt awkward at first. I understood it well because of Mumma, who seemed to only know patois, but I never spoke it on the regular. For weeks, I paced my apartment in L.A. chatting to myself, pronouncing every word slowly like I was rehearsing a song. *Why does it feel like this doesn't belong to me?* I thought.

I brought my insecurity about patois back to Jamaica with me—pacing around my kitchen in Montego Bay with the same anxiety. Surely, the Jamaicans who've been here their whole lives would find me out. "Fahrinnah," they'd yell and ship me back to the States. But Dad reassured me. "Yuh soun' good, mahn."

I asked him the same question I asked Cousin Delroy in the summer. Did he think I'd have a hard time being welcomed? I reminded him of those childhood trips to the island where my native cousins called us *yankie*.

"Yuh muss' ahnnastan' someting, Chooch," he said. "When dem' call yuh 'fahrinnah,' dem no mean seh yuh is an outsidah. Becaw when dem see an Englishmahn, dem nuh call 'im 'fahrinnah.' Dem call him 'English.' An' when dem see German, dem call him a 'German.' But when dem see you dem call yuh 'fahrinnah' becaw dem a say, 'Yuh a one a wi, but yuh did bahn a fahrin.'" This was news to me—good news.

"Chooch, yuh is a Jamaican," he emphasized. "Yuh jus' bahn een di U.S."

My father and I talk for hours when we're on the phone, and it always somehow gets really deep. We talk about religion, Black liberation, economics, and politics. But one of Dad's favorite topics is our own ancestry. My father is a proud descendant of the Maroons, Africans who escaped Spanish enslavement and established their own free communities in Jamaica's mountains. Not only that, but when Britain wrested control of the island from Spain, they waged war on the Maroons, seeking to enslave them, and lost. To this day, the Maroon towns live under different laws than the rest of the island. Dad always ended up retelling the story of his fierce ancestors. "It's in your blood," he'd often say to me. But it wasn't until I came back to Jamaica as a fugitive from American anti-Blackness that he really began to unpack what he meant by "it."

He began telling me about my great-grandfather, how he had been a writer like me. He also opened up a bit more about his own past as an anti-imperialist community organizer, a Garveyite through and through. He recounted his own spiritual journey— he felt so close to God as a young man that he levitated while meditating, twice, but he eventually witnessed too much injustice in the church to go on believing in organized religion. To this day he believes in a higher power—"The Most High," he calls Them—but remains an impassioned critic of Christendom.

He wanted me to know that I was part of this legacy, that my ability to think and write, my love of the arts, and my rebellious spirit were gifts from my ancestors. That the things I was doing now—my music, my writing, my work in the movement—were part of a larger story. "Mi a tell you dem ting yah so you cyan see dat yuh nuh come out mysteriously like so. Dem ting deh coom een fram fi yuh ancestah dem. Yuh annastan?"

"Yah mahn," I responded.

For days, I thought about the fact that my mother's bloodline could be traced all the way back to a white slaveholder and an African woman. There was so much I wanted to know about that woman, about Bid'ah. Was she an enslaved person? Was her relationship with the Scotsman consensual? But if there are any records of Bid'ah's life floating out there in the world, they're nearly impossible to find. History has been far more interested in Pennycook, the Scotsman, than in the people he owned.

I wish I could have just asked Bid'ah—or my mom. Mackie was probably the last person on the planet to know much about this ancestor. My mom dedicated her life to tracing our family tree; it's why she used to take us to Jamaica every two years. She wanted us to know our family there, connect to our heritage and culture, and to the land. I wished I could have asked Mackie about Bid'ah.

Then it occurred to me that I could. I'd heard many of my Black friends mention asking the ancestors for help. In fact, some of my closest friends encouraged me to ask the ancestors to help me write this book. But I'd been nowhere near ready to set up an altar and light candles to call on them. There are some boundaries that have been programmed into my body from growing up Evangelical in the shadow of Confederate Mount Rushmore, talking to the dead being one of them. Yet, at the same time, I could feel my heart reaching out to Bid'ah as I washed dishes in my Mobay apartment—an involuntary action, as natural as breathing or digestion. Suddenly, a thought flashed through my head like lightning—in patois no less: *A who teach wi fi treat fi wi ol' head dem like stranjah?* (Translation: Who taught us to treat our ancestors like strangers?)

In my heart, I knew the colonizer was the answer to that question. The colonizers were the ones who intentionally sought to sever the ties between our ancestors and ourselves. They're the ones who ripped babies from their mothers' arms and sold them to work camps hundreds of miles away; the ones who broke up spouses; who made our mother tongues illegal and refused to teach us to write in theirs, so our families would be impossible to reunite; it was they who imposed their last names on us to bury the trail back to Africa.

I could theorize here about why the colonizers took such great measures to estrange us from our ancestors, but those books have already been written. I want to emphasize how it felt for that question to descend on me in patois: "A who teach wi fi treat fi wi ol' head dem like stranjah?" I realized I didn't know why dividing us from our ancestors was so important to colonizers, but the fact that it was important to them suggests that ancestral links are powerful. In that moment, I realized I still had so much to unlearn—beginning with the colonizer's language.

In *Black Skin, White Masks*, Frantz Fanon makes the issue of language his first order of revolutionary business. "A man who possesses a language possesses as an indirect consequence the world expressed and implied by its language." Fanon was born on the Antillean island of Martinique, a colony of France. "The more a black Antillean assimilates the French language," he wrote, "the whiter he gets."[1]

My father seemed to echo this as we chatted patois together. "Patois is fi wi freedom," he said. I didn't really understand him at first. I'd always thought of patois as just "broken English," like many people do. Cousin Delroy had said as much. Over drinks at my favorite bar in Mobay, he asked: "Yuh know wha patois is?" I waited for him to tell me. "Di African people couldn't pronounce di English wuhd dem, so dem bruk it up." That's how so many people think of patois, but the more I practiced with my father the less satisfying that explanation became.

It must be partly true that the language of the British colonizers seemed strange to their African captives. But we have to keep in mind that English was being imposed on them and, at the same time, being withheld from them in the prohibition against reading. The colonizers seemed to only want their captives to know so much English. And it's likely that our ancestors weren't that interested in talking like—or with—their oppressors anyway. I think it's more likely that our ancestors learned enough English to communicate with them but were more content to create a language system that made it easier to communicate among themselves.

One of my favorite stories about my Jamaican ancestors is a trick they used on white Christian missionaries. Christianity had been a hard sell for enslaved Africans in the Colony of Jamaica, because the preachers used it to encourage submission to oppression. But my ancestors were shrewd. "You have a funny accent that's hard to understand," they'd tell the missionary. "We'd like to stay here a little while and help translate the message for the slower learners." Once the missionary was out of sight, they'd start freedom planning in patois. That strategy is partly how Baptist deacon Samuel Sharpe was able to organize thirty thousand enslaved people to launch an eleven-day rebellion on Christmas Day 1831.[2]

Patois isn't primitive or unsophisticated. It has rules just like any other language, and if you don't know the rules, it can be hard to follow. Only white arrogance convinced slaveholders that their prisoners resorted to "bastardized English" or gibberish out of a lack of intelligence, while thinking their own inability to understand patois betrayed no signal about their own aptitude. And the colonizers' arrogance allowed the enslaved to plan revolutions right under the so-called masters' noses. For that reason, I've come to appreciate my ancestors' language more than ever.

You don't learn patois from a book. You learn by speaking it with others. It's an embodied process engaged in community. And historically, it's been a way to rebel against white power— the power to define who has attained humanity, and therefore human rights, through the signal of speech. It felt so transgressive to break the rules of the language I'd been reared in as a boy. But the more I chat patois with my father, the more liberating it felt. And in learning to chat patois, I was unlearning values and norms we don't often consciously think of in English: most notably, what does the speech of an intelligent man sound like? In America, many people curl their lips at people who "sound ghetto" because they use African American Vernacular English (also known as "Ebonics"), but that's just a cultural way we reinforce white supremacist norms. White people don't have a monopoly on intelligent speech—or, by extension, on intelligent people.

Within weeks, I was waking up to my inner monologue in patois. It made my brain hurt at first, but once I got used to the fact that the person speaking in my head in patois is me, I realized something profound about what it meant to embrace my ancestors' language. I wasn't just internalizing vowel pronunciations. I was becoming someone else—myself of course, but a different edition. I wondered about all the things this other, patois-speaking Andre had to say.

All along, there had been a person underneath all the habits and values formed by white society in me. Now he was beginning to emerge, like the first tiny leaf breaking through the soil in spring. As I settled into life in Mobay and thought about the many questions I might encounter on the road ahead, I felt aware of all I'd already unlearned over the six years I've recounted in this book.

At the beginning of my journey, I needed to find the courage to call bullshit on the white world's racial gaslighting and accept my lived experience in this Black body as a credible source of knowledge. The political dimensions of our personal experiences had to be made clear to me, and revolution went from sounding like an extreme idea to the only legitimate response to systemic racism. To pursue that revolution, I had to be liberated from the lie that I owe white supremacists—even benevolent, unintentional ones—an audience or platform for their nonsense. I discovered the power of being divisive, and my definition of hope grew deeper than unmerited optimism and hollow sentimentality, to something robust and anchored in history. Most important of all, I came to know the importance of Black joy. Black people deserve more than struggle—we deserve to enjoy our lives without fear, just like anyone else.

In a way, the apocalypse revealed to me that I was also one of the white friends I couldn't keep—by which I mean the Andre they had trained to abide by white norms. I come from the stock of Maroon warriors and insurgent pastors. I was born to rebel, but white lies were sewn into my nervous system, telling my Maroon rebel self that he's not free to walk freely through this world in all his terrifying glory. Those lies once surrounded me like prison bars, confining me to the kind of Black man they can be comfortable around. But I'm not their captive anymore. To borrow a term from the churches that raised me, I am being born again.

Many Black people have such a person we're learning to leave behind: the identity shaped and defined by the judgment and policing of the white world. The same goes for indigenous people and people of color. If that's you, I hope you found something of use in this book.

Forgive me for digging into my theology bag again for a second, but it's the best analogy I have. In the Hebrew Bible, there's a word used for salvation that means "to take from an enclosed space to a wide-open space." That's how I've come to see my journey of breaking free from the colonizer's control. For centuries now, whiteness has been presented to us as a road to salvation. We've been told how to talk, pray, wear our clothes, express our feelings, and so much more—enclosed in the tiny hole whiteness has carved for us, like the ones they shoved us into on their slave vessels. But we've always sought the wide-open space where the definitions of truth, dignity, and who is worthy of care are not the prerogative of a privileged few. Today I hear a voice—maybe it's the voice of John, who first envisioned these words on the lips of angels laying waste to the oppressive Roman empire, or the sound of Rastaman dem a sing to di heaven, or the voice of my dad or Bid'ah, or the Most High Godself. I can hear it calling me—and maybe, if you listen, you can hear it calling, too.

"Come out of Babylon," it says to us all. "Come out into the wide-open space."

ACKNOWLEDGMENTS

The president of my alma mater, Dr. Mark Rutland, often told the following proverb: "If you ever see a turtle on a fence post, you can be sure he didn't get there all by himself." His point was that there's often a community of people who help us accomplish great things. I acknowledge that I am a turtle on a fence post, and there are so many people I need to thank for the contributions they've made to my growth as a writer and artist that brought me here.

Thank you, Dominique Robinson and Tamisha Tyler, for telling me that I needed to write and take my ideas seriously.

Thank you, Lauralee Farrer, Paul Corrigan, Rose Gwynn, Toby Castle, and Rachel Paprocki, for reading and editing so many early drafts of my writing.

Thank you, Steve Ross, for taking a chance on me.

Thank you to my Black delegation—Tina Strawn, Dante Stewart, Deborah Masten, Taeshia Ageymang, and Nandi K.—for your early feedback on the early drafts of this book.

Thank you to all of my collaborators from A Subversive Liturgy, Good Trouble Pasadena, and Black Lives Matter Pasadena, for your camaraderie and great memories.

Thank you, Amy Tahani-Bidmeshki, for challenging the way I think, even if we don't always agree.

Thank you, Srdja Popovic and Bob Helvey, for welcoming me as a student and friend.

Thank you to the Freedom Global Writers Group for providing a weekly space for me to work on the many drafts of this book.

Finally, thank you to my family, for always loving and supporting me no matter what.

NOTES

1. EMBRACING THE APOCALYPSE

1. David DeSilva, "The 'Image of the Beast' and the Christians in Asia Minor: Escalation of Sectarian Tension in Revelation 13," *Trinity Journal* 12, no. 2 (1991): 185–208. galaxie.com/article/trinj12-2-05.
2. Stephanie Muravchik and Jon A. Shields, "Commentary: Why Trump Made Gains Among Minority Men Against Biden," *Fortune,* November 6, 2020; accessed June 18, 2021, fortune.com/2020/11/06/trump-support-black-latino-men-rappers/.

2. THE WHOLE WORLD IS STONE MOUNTAIN

1. Eric Williams, "British Industry and the Triangular Trade," in *Capitalism and Slavery* (Chapel Hill: University of North Carolina Press, 2014).
2. Lauren Collins, "The Haitian Revolution and the Hole in French High-School History," *The New Yorker*, December 3, 2020; accessed August 10, 2021, newyorker.com/culture/culture-desk/the-haitian-revolution-and-the-hole-in-french-high-school-history.

3. Kate Shuster, "Teaching the Hard History of American Slavery," Southern Poverty Law Center, January 31, 2018; accessed May 17, 2021, splcenter.org/teaching-hard-history-american-slavery.

4. Doug McAdam, "The Political Process Model," in *Political Process and the Development of Black Insurgency: 1930–1970* (Chicago: University of Chicago Press, 1990), 34.

5. Rick Perlstein, "Exclusive: Lee Atwater's Infamous 1981 Interview on the Southern Strategy," *The Nation,* November 13, 2012, youtube.com/watch?v=X_8E3ENrKrQ.

6. Ashley Southall and Michael Gold, "Why 'Stop-and-Frisk' Inflamed Black and Hispanic Neighborhoods," *The New York Times,* November 17, 2019; accessed June 18, 2021, nytimes.com/2019/11/17/nyregion/bloomberg-stop-and-frisk-new-york.html.

7. Paul Butler, *Chokehold: Policing Black Men* (New York: New Press, 2018), 81.

8. Josh Sanburn, "Behind the Video of Eric Garner's Deadly Confrontation With New York Police," *Time,* July 23, 2014; accessed August 10, 2021, time.com/3016326/eric-garner-video-police-chokehold-death/.

9. "Why Freddie Gray Ran," editorial, *The Baltimore Sun,* April 25, 2015; accessed May 31, 2019, baltimoresun.com/opinion/editorial/bs-ed-freddie-gray-20150425-story.html.

10. Susan York Morris, "Gaslighting: Signs and Tips for Seeking Help," *Healthline,* April 1, 2017; accessed June 18, 2021, healthline.com/health/gaslighting.

11. York Morris, "Gaslighting."

12. Mark Engler and Paul Engler, "Introduction," in *This Is an Uprising: How Nonviolent Revolt Is Shaping the Twenty-First Century* (New York: Bold Type Books, 2017), ix.

13. Mahatma Gandhi, *Non-Violent Resistance (Satyagraha)* (New York: Dover, 2001), 3.

3. THE RIGHT TO REMAIN ANGRY

1. Brett Weiner, "Verbatim: The Ferguson Case," *The New York Times,* YouTube, August 6, 2015, youtube.com/watch?v=pQXbEUEtf2U.

2. Conor Friedersdorf, "Witnesses Saw Michael Brown Attacking—and Others Saw Him Giving Up," *The Atlantic,* published November 25, 2014, accessed July 22, 2021, theatlantic.com/national/archive/2014/11/major-contradictions-in-eyewitness-accounts-of-michael-browns-death/383157/.

3. "10,000 Strong Peacefully Protest In Downtown Baltimore (Media Over-Reports Violence and Arrests)," *Good Black News,* published April 28, 2015; accessed July 22, 2021, goodblacknews.org/2015/04/27/10000-strong-peacefully-protest-in-downtown-baltimore-media-over-reports-violence-and-arrests/.

4. Annette Gordon-Reed and Winthrop D. Jordan, "Introduction," in *Slavery and the American South Essays and Commentaries* (Jackson: University Press of Mississippi, 2003), xv.

5. Drew Magary, "Duck Dynasty's Phil Robertson Gives Drew Magary a Tour of West Monroe," *GQ,* December 17, 2013; accessed May 17, 2021, gq.com/story/duck-dynasty-phil-robertson.

6. *What Happened, Miss Simone?,* directed by Liz Garbus (Radical Media, 2015).

7. *What Happened, Miss Simone?*

8. "Malcolm X's Fiery Speech Addressing Police Brutality," Smithsonian Channel, YouTube, February 16, 2018, youtube.com/watch?v=6_uYWDyYNUg.

9. "William H. Grier and Price M. Cobbs on 'Black Rage' (1968)," reel-black, YouTube, January 16, 2020; accessed July 30, 2021, youtube.com/watch?v=gdbTJiMwUhQ.

10. "To Be in a Rage, Almost All the Time," 1A podcast, National Public Radio, June 1, 2020; accessed June 18, 2021, npr.org/2020/06/01/867153918/-to-be-in-a-rage-almost-all-the-time.

11. Brian Martin, "Backfire: Basics," in *Backfire Manual: Tactics Against Injustice* (Sparsnäs: Irene Publishing, 2012), 8.

12. "1966: Stokeley Carmichael, 'Black Power,'" *BlackPast,* July 13, 2020; accessed June 18, 2021, blackpast.org/african-american-history/speeches -african-american-history/1966-stokely-carmichael-black-power.

4. THE PERSONAL AND THE POLITICAL

1. "Brenda Eichelberger," *Wikipedia,* en.wikipedia.org/wiki/Brenda_ Eichelberger#cite_note-:2-3.
2. Keeanga-Yamahtta Taylor, ed., *How We Get Free: Black Feminism and the Combahee River Collective* (Chicago: Haymarket Books, 2017).
3. Assata Shakur, *Assata: an Autobiography* (Westport, Conn.: Lawrence Hill, 2001), 542.
4. Linda Napikoski, "Feminist Consciousness-Raising Groups and Women's History," *ThoughtCo.,* October 14, 2019; accessed May 17, 2021, thoughtco.com/feminist-consciousness-raising-groups-3528954.
5. Kimberlé Crenshaw, "Mapping the Margins: Intersectionality, Identity Politics, and Violence Against Women of Color," *Stanford Law Review* 43, no. 6 (1991): 1241–1299, jstor.org/stable/1229039.
6. Aric McBay, "The Making of a Radical," in *Full Spectrum Resistance, Volume 1: Building Movements and Fighting to Win* (New York: Seven Stories Press, 2019), 311.
7. "An Empire of Slavery and the Consumer Revolution," Lumen, accessed June 18, 2021, courses.lumenlearning.com/atd-sanjac-ushistory1/ chapter/an-empire-of-slavery-and-the-consumer-revolution.
8. Paul Gorski, "Consumerism as Racial and Economic Injustice: The Macroaggressions that Make Me, and Maybe You, a Hypocrite," *Understanding and Dismantling Privilege* 4, no. 1 (2013), 1–21; accessed June 18, 2021, researchgate.net/publication/260985713_Consumerism _as_Racial_and_Economic_Injustice_The_Macroaggressions_that _Make_Me_and_Maybe_You_a_Hypocrite.
9. Ben Kesslen, "Video Shows White Men in N.J. Mocking George Floyd's Death at Protest," NBC News, June 10, 2020; accessed June 18,

2021, nbcnews.com/news/us-news/video-shows-white-men-n-j-mocking -george-floyd-s-n1229051.

10. Gene Demby, "For People of Color, a Housing Market Partially Hidden From View," National Public Radio, June 17, 2013; accessed June 18, 2021, npr.org/sections/codeswitch/2013/06/17/192730233/ for-people-of-color-a-housing-market-partially-hidden-from-view.

5. WE DO NOT DEBATE WITH RACISTS

1. NewsOne staff, "Dispatch Call Reveals Cop Pulled Philando Castile Over for 'Wide Set Nose,'" *NewsOne,* July 10, 2016; accessed June 19, 2021, newsone.com/3478387/police-audio-philando-castile-wide-set -nose/.

2. Marina Koren, "Why the Stanford Judge Gave Brock Turner Six Months," *The Atlantic,* June 17, 2016; accessed June 18, 2021, theatlantic.com/news/archive/2016/06/stanford-rape-case-judge/487415/.

3. Ben Leonard, "'QAnon Shaman' Granted Organic Food in Jail after Report of Deteriorating Health," Politico, February 3, 2021; accessed June 20, 2021, politico.com/news/2021/02/03/qanon-shaman-organic -food-465563. I'm not arguing that Jacob Chansley's dietary needs should have been ignored. My point is that if he had been Black they probably *would have been* ignored.

4. Gabriel L. Schwartz and Jaquelyn L. Jahn, "Mapping Fatal Police Violence Across U.S. Metropolitan Areas: Overall Rates of Racial/Ethnic Inequities, 2013–2017," *PLOS One* 15, no. 6 (2020): 1–16, published June 24, 2020; accessed June 18, 2021, journals.plos.org/plosone/ article?id=10.1371/journal.pone.0229686.

5. Eyder Peralta and Cheryl Corley, "The Driving Life and Death of Philando Castile," *Morning Edition,* National Public Radio, July 15, 2016; accessed June 18, 2021, npr.org/sections/thetwo-way/2016/07/15/ 485835272/the-driving-life-and-death-of-philando-castile.

6. David Robson, "The '3.5% Rule': How a Small Minority Can Change the World," BBC Future, May 13, 2019; accessed June 19, 2021, bbc

.com/future/article/20190513-it-only-takes-35-of-people-to-change-the-world.

6. WE CAN ALL BE WHITE

1. Randall M. Miller, "The Man in the Middle: The Black Slave Driver," *American Heritage* 30 no. 6 (October/November 1979); accessed June 18, 2021, americanheritage.com/man-middle.

2. Willie Jennings, "Can 'White' People Be Saved: Reflections on Missions and Whiteness," Fuller Seminary, YouTube, February 24, 2018; accessed June 19, 2021, youtube.com/watch?v=SRLjWZxL1lE.

3. Beverly Daniel Tatum, "Defining Racism: 'Can We Talk,'" in *Why Are All the Black Kids Sitting Together in the Cafeteria? And Other Conversations About Race* (New York: Perseus Books, 2003), 156.

4. Solomon Jones, "The Frightening Effectiveness of Black Sellouts like Candace Owens," *The Philadelphia Inquirer,* March 20, 2019; accessed June 18, 2021, inquirer.com/opinion/candace-owens-new-zealand-mosque-trump-20190319.html.

5. Srdja Popovic and Matthew Miller, "The Almighty Pillars of Power," in *Blueprint for Revolution: How to Use Rice Pudding, Lego Men, and Other Nonviolent Techniques to Galvanize Communities, Overthrow Dictators, or Simply Change the World* (New York: Spiegel & Grau, 2015), 108.

6. "The Chairman Fred Hampton," Incarcerated Nation Network, YouTube, December 4, 2020, youtube.com/watch?v=S3mungAFfoc.

7. Martin Luther King, Jr., "Pilgrimage to Nonviolence," in *The Radical King,* edited by Cornel West (Boston: Beacon Press, 2016), 79.

8. Peter Mitchell, "To the Far Right, Attacks on Protesters as Enemies of 'Western Culture' Are a Gift," *The Guardian,* June 10, 2020; accessed June 18, 2021, theguardian.com/commentisfree/2020/jun/10/attacks-protesters-enemies-western-culture-traction-far-right.

9. Caleb Ecarma, Eric Lutz, and Bess Levin, "White Nationalists Sure Don't Think Tucker Carlson's 'Replacement' Segment Is About Voting Rights," *Vanity Fair,* April 14, 2021; accessed June 19, 2021,

vanityfair.com/news/2021/04/white-nationalists-tucker-carlsons
-replacement.

10. Erica Chenoweth and Maria J. Stephan, *Why Civil Resistance Works:
the Strategic Logic of Nonviolent Conflict* (New York: Columbia University Press, 2013), 476.

7. BREAKING UP WITH WHITE JESUS

1. Willie James Jennings, *The Christian Imagination: Theology and the
Origins of Race* (New Haven, Conn.: Yale University Press, 2011), 79.

2. DeNeen L. Brown, "The Preacher Who Used Christianity to Revive
the Ku Klux Klan," *The Washington Post,* June 12, 2020; accessed
June 18, 2021, washingtonpost.com/news/retropolis/wp/2018/04/08/
the-preacher-who-used-christianity-to-revive-the-ku-klux-klan/.

3. Wyatte Grantham-Philips, "Pastor Paula White Calls on Angels from
Africa and South America to Bring Trump Victory," *USA Today,* November 6, 2020; accessed June 18, 2021, usatoday.com/story/news/
nation/2020/11/05/paula-white-trumps-spiritual-adviser-african
-south-american-angels/6173576002/; Matt Gutman, "Crowds Protest
Outside Election Headquarters in Nevada," ABC News, November 5,
2020; accessed June 19, 2021, yahoo.com/gma/crowds-protest-outside
-election-headquarters-225551246.html.

4. Yonat Shimron, "Southern Baptist Seminary Presidents Nix Critical
Race Theory," *Religion News Service,* December 2, 2020; accessed
June 18, 2021, religionnews.com/2020/12/01/southern-baptist-seminary
-presidents-nix-critical-race-theory/.

5. "In U.S., Decline of Christianity Continues at Rapid Pace," Pew
Research Center, October 17, 2019; accessed June 18, 2021, pew
forum.org/2019/10/17/in-u-s-decline-of-christianity-continues-at-rapid
-pace.

6. "The Gospel and Black Lives Matter—John MacArthur," Christian
Defense International, YouTube, July 13, 2018; accessed June 19,
2021, youtube.com/watch?v=pkOv94cyfc4.

7. German Lopez, "Charlotte Police Officer Who Shot and Killed Keith

Lamont Scott Will Not Face Charges," *Vox,* September 21, 2016; accessed June 18, 2021, vox.com/2016/9/21/12999366/keith-lamont-scott-north-carolina-police-shooting.

8. Michael Eli Dokosi, "How England's First Slave Trader Lured Africans on His 'Jesus' Ship and Sold Them into Slavery," *Face2face Africa,* October 11, 2019; accessed June 18, 2021, face2faceafrica.com/article/how-englands-first-slave-trader-lured-africans-on-his-jesus-ship-and-sold-them-into-slavery12.

9. Angela Jones, "Frederick Douglass: American Slavery," in *The Modern African American Thought Reader: From David Walker to Barack Obama* (New York: Routledge, 2012), 48–50.

10. Shakur, *Assata,* 532.

11. Paul Caron, "Michelle Alexander Resigns From Ohio State Law Faculty for Seminary, Valuing 'Publicly Accessible Writing Over Academic Careerism'; Law Without 'A Moral Or Spiritual Awakening' Cannot Bring About Justice," *Taxprof Blog,* September 25, 2016; accessed June 18, 2021, taxprof.typepad.com/taxprof_blog/2016/09/michelle-alexander-resigns-from-ohio-state-law-faculty-for-seminary-valuing-publicly-accessible-writ.html#more.

12. Micah White, "Mental Environmentalism," in *The End of Protest: a New Playbook for Revolution* (Toronto: Knopf Canada, 2016), 236.

8. REVOLUTION NOW

1. Pamela Engel, "Former KKK Leader David Duke: 'Our People Have Played a HUGE Role in Electing Trump!'" *Business Insider,* November 9, 2016; accessed June 19, 2021, businessinsider.com/david-duke-kkk-trump-election-2016-11.

2. Sonia Chopra, "Watch Eddie Huang Eat Dinner with a White Nationalist," *Eater,* August 16, 2017; accessed June 18, 2021, eater.com/2017/8/16/16155996/eddie-huang-white-nationalist-dinner.

3. Scott Clement and Max Ehrenfreund, "Economic and Racial Anxiety: Two Separate Forces Driving Support for Donald Trump," *The Washington Post,* April 29, 2019; accessed June 19, 2021, washingtonpost

.com/news/wonk/wp/2016/03/22/economic-anxiety-and-racial-anxiety
-two-separate-forces-driving-support-for-donald-trump/.

4. Philip Klinkner, "The Easiest Way to Guess If Someone Supports
Trump? Ask If Obama Is a Muslim," *Vox,* June 2, 2016; accessed
June 19, 2021, vox.com/2016/6/2/11833548/donald-trump-support
-race-religion-economy.

5. Emma Green, "It Was Cultural Anxiety That Drove White, Working-
Class Voters to Trump," *The Atlantic,* May 12, 2017; accessed June 19,
2021, theatlantic.com/politics/archive/2017/05/white-working-class
-trump-cultural-anxiety/525771/.

6. James Q. Whitman, "The First Nuremburg Law," in *Hitler's American
Model: The United States and the Making of Nazi Race Law* (Princeton, N.J.: Princeton University Press, 2017), 43.

7. Langston Hughes, "Too Much of Race," in *The Collected Works
of Langston Hughes, vol. 10: Fight for Freedom and Other Writings on Civil Rights* (Columbia: University of Missouri Press, 2001),
221.

8. Martin Luther King, Jr., "Where Are We?" in *Where Do We Go from
Here: Chaos or Community?* (Boston: Beacon Press, 2010), 41.

9. Kathleen Cleaver, "Racism, Fascism, and Political Murder," in *The
U.S. Antifascism Reader,* eds. Bill V. Mullen and Christopher Vials
(New York: Verso Books, 2020), 538–51.

10. Bill Mullen and Chris Vials, "Introduction: Anti/Fascism and the
United States," in *The U.S. Antifascism Reader,* 19–61.

11. Louie Dean Valencia-García, "This Is American Fascism," *Open Democracy,* January 14, 2021; accessed June 18, 2021, opendemocracy
.net/en/countering-radical-right/american-fascism/.

12. Gary May, "A Revolution of Values: Martin Luther King Jr. and the
Poor People's Campaign," billmoyers.com, August 31, 2020; accessed
June 18, 2021, billmoyers.com/2015/01/18/revolution-values/.

13. "MLK Talks 'New Phase' of Civil Rights Struggle, 11 Months Before
His Assassination," NBC News, April 4, 2018; accessed July 28, 2021,
youtube.com/watch?v=2xsbt3a7K-8.

9. (WHITE) MEN EXPLAIN THINGS TO ME

1. James Q. Wilson and George L. Kelling, "Broken Windows," *The Atlantic,* July 20, 2020; accessed June 18, 2021, theatlantic.com/magazine/archive/1982/03/broken-windows/304465/.

2. Christina Cauterucci, "Korryn Gaines Is the Ninth Black Woman Shot and Killed by Police in the U.S. This Year," *Slate,* August 3, 2016; accessed June 18, 2021, slate.com/human-interest/2016/08/korryn-gaines-is-the-ninth-black-woman-shot-and-killed-by-police-in-the-u-s-this-year.html.

3. Jacqui Germain, "On Korryn Gaines and Black Women Who Dare to Be Defiant," *Feministing,* 2017; accessed June 19, 2021, feministing.com/2016/08/04/on-korryn-gaines-and-black-women-who-dare-to-be-defiant/.

4. Noura Erakat and Paul C. Gorski, "Racism, Whiteness, and Burnout in Antiracism Movements: How White Racial Justice Activists Elevate Burnout in Racial Justice Activists of Color in the United States," *Ethnicities* 19, no. 5 (2019): 784–808; accessed May 17, 2021, journals.sagepub.com/doi/full/10.1177/1468796819833871.

5. Doug McAdam, "Freedom High: The Summer of '64," in *Freedom Summer* (New York: Oxford University Press, 1988), 101–15.

6. Andre Henry, "Decentering Whiteness with No White Saviors Part 1," *Hope and Hard Pills,* April 17, 2020; accessed July 31, 2021, hope-hard-pills.simplecast.com/episodes/decentering-whiteness-with-no-white-saviors-part-1.

10. HOW TO BE HOPEFUL

1. Cleve R. Wootson Jr., et al., "Texas Police Officer Who Killed Black Teen Could Spend Rest of His Life in Prison," *The Washington Post,* May 7, 2017; accessed June 18, 2021, washingtonpost.com/news/post-nation/wp/2017/05/06/texas-police-officer-who-killed-black-teen-could-spend-rest-of-his-life-in-prison/.

2. Rebecca Solnit, "Foreword to the Third Edition," in *Hope in the Dark: Untold Histories, Wild Possibilities* (Chicago: Haymarket Books, 2016), 12.

3. McAdam, "The Political Process Model," 36–60.

4. Doug McAdam, "The Historical Context of Black Insurgency: 1876–1954," in *Political Process and the Development of Black Insurgency: 1930–1970* (Chicago: University of Chicago Press, 1990), 65–116.

11. THE TRUTH ABOUT UNITY

1. Carrie Dann, "NBC/WSJ Poll: Majority Say Kneeling During Anthem 'Not Appropriate,'" NBC News, August 31, 2018; accessed June 20, 2021, nbcnews.com/politics/first-read/nbc-wsj-poll-majority-say -kneeling-during-anthem-not-appropriate-n904891.

2. "Trump: NFL Kneelers 'Maybe Shouldn't Be in Country,'" BBC, May 24, 2018; accessed June 18, 2021, bbc.com/news/world-us -canada-44232979.

3. Chenoweth and Stephan, *Why Civil Resistance Works*.

4. Mark Engler and Paul Engler, "Introduction," in *This Is an Uprising: How Nonviolent Revolt Is Shaping the Twenty-first Century* (New York: Bold Type Books, 2017), 12-34.

5. Donald L. Grant and Johnathan Grant, "The Civil Rights Movement," in *The Way It Was in the South: The Black Experience in Georgia* (Athens: University of Georgia Press, 2001), 30.

6. Srdja Popovic and Matthew Miller, "The Almighty Pillars of Power," in *Blueprint for Revolution: How to Use Rice Pudding, Lego Men, and Other Nonviolent Techniques to Galvanize Communities, Overthrow Dictators, or Simply Change the World* (New York: Spiegel & Grau, 2015).

7. Gene Sharp, *Power and Struggle* (Boston: Porter Sargent, 1973).

8. Mark Engler and Paul Engler, "The Dividers," in *This Is an Uprising: How Nonviolent Revolt Is Shaping the Twenty-First Century* (New York: Bold Type Books, 2017), 367–414.

9. adrienne maree brown, "Unthinkable Thoughts," in *We Will Not Cancel Us and Other Dreams of Transformative Justice* (Edinburgh: AK Press, 2021), 33–64.

10. "(1857) Frederick Douglass, 'If There Is No Struggle, There Is No Progress,'" *BlackPast,* January 25, 2007; accessed June 20, 2021, blackpast.org/african-american-history/1857-frederick-douglass-if-there-no-struggle-there-no-progress/.

11. "Martin Luther King Jr. 'Birth of a New Nation' April 7, 1957," nicholasflyer, YouTube, September 24, 2015; accessed June 20, 2021, youtube.com/watch?v=O1QaSFm6Hhk.

12. Kenrya Rankin, "Alicia Garza on Importance of Voting, Disruptive Black Power," *ColorLines,* June 22, 2016; accessed June 20, 2021, colorlines.com/articles/alicia-garza-importance-voting-disruptive-black-power.

12. BUILDING OUR OWN TABLES

1. Glenn E. Bracey II and Wendy Leo Moore, "'Race Tests': Racial Boundary Maintenance in White Evangelical Churches," *Sociological Inquiry* 87, no. 2 (2017): 282–302; accessed August 4, 2021, researchgate.net/publication/316355727_Race_Tests_Racial_Boundary_Maintenance_in_White_Evangelical_Churches/.

2. Kate Duffy, "A Black Ex-Googler Claimed She Was Told by a Manager That Her Baltimore-Accented Speech Was a 'Disability' and Later Fired," *Business Insider,* December 22, 2020; accessed June 20, 2021, businessinsider.com/google-fired-employee-diversity-recruiter-baltimore-accent-was-disability-2020-12.

3. Cade Metz and Daisuke Wakabayashi, "Google Researcher Says She Was Fired over Paper Highlighting Bias in A.I.," *The New York Times,* December 3, 2020; accessed June 20, 2021, nytimes.com/2020/12/03/technology/google-researcher-timnit-gebru.html.

4. Jason Del Rey, "Bias, Disrespect, and Demotions: Black Employees Say Amazon Has a Race Problem," *Vox,* February 26, 2021; accessed

June 18, 2021, vox.com/recode/2021/2/26/22297554/amazon-race
-black-diversity-inclusion.

5. Catherine H. Augustine et al., "Can Restorative Practices Improve
School Climate and Curb Suspensions?" RAND Corporation, December 27, 2018; accessed June 18, 2021, rand.org/pubs/research
_reports/RR2840.html.

6. Senay Bostaz, "Why Are There So Few Prisoners in the Netherlands?" *The Guardian,* December 12, 2019; accessed June 18, 2021,
theguardian.com/world/2019/dec/12/why-are-there-so-few-prisoners
-in-the-netherlands.

7. Rick Noack and Karla Adam, "Defund the Police? Other Countries
Have Narrowed Their Role and Boosted Other Services," *The Washington Post*; accessed July 31, 2021, washingtonpost.com/world/
europe/police-protests-countries-reforms/2020/06/13/596eab16-abf2
-11ea-a43b-be9f6494a87d_story.html.

13. HOW BLACK LOVE BECAME IMPORTANT TO ME

1. "Hella LA," *Insecure,* season 2, episode 4, directed by Prentice Penny.

2. Nigel Roberts, "Jeezy Says He and Jeannie Mai Discussed Her Offensive Comment About Black Men," BET, November 21, 2020; accessed December 8, 2022, bet.com/article/u5s0va/jeezy-and-jeannie
-mai-discussed-offensive-comment.

3. Linda Ikeji, "Private Group Chat of White Women Shaming and Be-
littling Black Men Leaks," *Linda Ikeji's Blog,* December 13, 2020;
accessed June 18, 2021, lindaikejisblog.com/2020/12/private-group-
chat-of-white-women-shaming-and-belittling-black-men-leaks.html.

4. Frank B. Wilderson III, "Hattie McDaniel Is Dead," in *Afropessimism* (New York: Liveright, 2021), 62.

5. Gina Torino, "How Racism and Microaggressions Lead to Worse
Health," Center for Health Journalism, November 10, 2017; accessed
June 19, 2021, centerforhealthjournalism.org/2017/11/08/how-racism
-and-microaggressions-lead-worse-health.

6. Torino, "How Racism and Microaggressions Lead to Worse Health."

7. Ibram X. Kendi, "Biology," in *How to Be an Antiracist* (New York: One World, 2019), 93–120.

14. TO FIGHT OR TO FLEE

1. Zak Cheney-Rice, "Georgia Is Really Good at Making It Hard for Black People to Vote, Study Finds," *Intelligencer,* December 13, 2019; accessed June 20, 2021, nymag.com/intelligencer/2019/12/georgia-voter-suppression-under-kemp.html.

2. William Cummings, "Georgia Gubernatorial Candidate Brian Kemp Suggests Truck Is for Rounding Up 'Illegals,'" *USA Today,* May 10, 2018; accessed June 20, 2021, usatoday.com/story/news/nation/2018/05/10/brian-kemp-illegals-ad/600212002/.

3. Grace Panetta, "Trump Hints That He Could Refuse to Accept the Results of the 2020 Election If He Loses," *Business Insider,* July 19, 2020; accessed June 20, 2021, businessinsider.com/trump-suggests-that-he-wont-accept-the-2020-election-results-if-he-loses-2020-7.

4. Jemima McEvoy, "Trump-Ordered Federal Agents Are Reportedly Pulling Protesters Into Unmarked Vehicles, Drawing Outrage," *Forbes,* July 17, 2020; accessed June 20, 2021, forbes.com/sites/jemimamcevoy/2020/07/17/trump-ordered-federal-agents-are-reportedly-pulling-protesters-into-unmarked-vehicles-drawing-outrage/?sh=29a11c3a70de.

5. Yelena Dzhanova, "Kyle Rittenhouse's Mom Says Her Son Was 'Helping' Businesses and 'Protesters Should Not Have Been There,'" *Insider,* November 10, 2020; accessed June 18, 2021, insider.com/kyle-rittenhouses-mom-says-her-son-was-helping-businesses-2020-11.

6. Andre Henry, "Toppling a Dictator with Srdja Popovic," *Hope and Hard Pills* podcast, December 21, 2020; accessed June 20, 2021, hope-hard-pills.simplecast.com/episodes/creating-a-blueprint-for-revolution-with-srdja-popovic.

7. McAdam, "Freedom High."

15. BORN AGAIN

1. Frantz Fanon, "The Black Man and Language," in *Black Skin, White Masks* (New York: Grove Press, 2008), 28–63.
2. Noel Leo Erskine, "Rastafari Theology," in *From Garvey to Marley: Rastafari Theology* (Gainesville: University Press of Florida, 2007), 1–38.

ABOUT THE AUTHOR

ANDRE HENRY is an award-winning musician, writer, and activist contending for the world that ought to be. He's a student of nonviolent struggle, having organized protests in Los Angeles, where he lives, and having studied under international movement leaders through the Harvard Kennedy School. He is a columnist for Religion News Service and the author of the newsletter "Hope and Hard Pills." His activism in pursuit of racial justice has been featured in *The New Yorker*, *The Nation*, and on *The Liturgists Podcast*.

andrehenry.co
Facebook.com/theandrehenry
Instagram: @theandrehenry
Twitter: @andrehenry